Love Marriage & Money

Understanding and Achieving Financial Compatibility Before–and After–You Say "I Do"

Gail Liberman Alan Lavine

Dearborn
Financial Publishing, Inc.®

Editorial Director: Cynthia A. Zigmund
Managing Editor: Jack Kiburz
Interior Design: Lucy Jenkins
Cover Design: Design Alliance, Inc.
Typesetting: Professional Resources & Communications, Inc.

Library of Congress Cataloging-in-Publication Data

Liberman, Gail, 1951-
    Love, Marriage & Money: understanding and achieving financial compatibility before--and after--you say "I do" / Gail Liberman and Alan Lavine.
    p. cm.
    Includes Index.
    ISBN 0-7931-2661-4 (pbk.)
    1. Married people--Finance, Personal. 2. Finance, Personal. 3. Marriage. I. Lavine, Alan. II. Title.
HG179.L484 1998
332.024' 0655--dc21
                                                                        98-12784
                                                                             CIP

Dedication

To Si and Dorothy Liberman, who, for nearly a half century, have successfully met the challenges of love, marriage, and money. . . .

Other Books by Gail Liberman and Alan Lavine

The Complete Idiot's Guide to Making Money with Mutual Funds

Improving Your Credit and Reducing Your Debt

Other Books by Alan Lavine

50 Ways to Mutual Fund Profits

Getting Started in Mutual Funds

Your Life Insurance Options

Contents

Introduction

Married or not, you'll learn all too quickly how well you get along when the subject of money pops up. From day one when you go on your first date, money directly affects your attitudes toward each other.

As you'll see, we learned this lesson early on in our relationship. Nevertheless, getting along on the subject of money is only the tip of the iceberg. If you plan to stay together, both of you will have to agree on some very important financial issues. You don't have to be gurus at the Federal Reserve, but making these decisions smartly and together is critical. They not only will affect the standard of living you experience for years to come, but they'll also directly influence your overall happiness.

We're all not doing so well in this department, evidenced by numerous studies that peg money as the number one cause of arguments as well as the number one cause of divorce.

Sure, it's easy to say that if you have young children and are saving for retirement 25 years down the road, you need to put most of your savings in common stock funds for growth. But where do you get the extra money to save in the first place?

It's one thing to read about what you should do when it comes to managing your financial affairs, and another to agree on a course of action. And what you read in popular money magazines, newspapers, or books may be a heckuva lot different from what you wind up doing simply because you can't agree.

What about you? We'd be willing to bet that money issues have surfaced in your own relationship—no matter how young or old it is. Does the man or woman pick up the tab on a date? Who pays for the wedding? Does it really pay you financially to get married in the first place? Should a woman take her husband's name?

If you're living together or married already, there are decisions to be made about whether you should have joint checking accounts and in whose name your home and other investments should be held. Then, of course, you both need to live with the decisions. You certainly want to avoid those "Whose fault is it this time?" battles—no matter who messed up or at what stage of life your money woes hit.

Equality when it comes to financial decision-making is important, and this book seeks to help you balance the scales on money issues. Does one of you pay the bills, manage the money, and make all the decisions about insurance and other financial issues? If so, we're willing to wager that there's some festering hostility. One of you is bound to feel inferior or resentful! In fact, lawyers tell us that situations in which one spouse has no clue about how to manage money often can lead to divorce, as well as money problems afterward.

Like us, one of you might be a spender and the other a saver. Or maybe you both spend too much. We've been on both sides of the fence and believe us, we've had some awful fights about money. Fortunately, we've learned—and are still learning—to compromise.

It's tough. Like many couples, each of us in a relationship has his or her own way of doing things. We've learned to make decisions together—well, almost. However, we also have learned that you just can't snap your fingers and *voila!* everything is all right. Financial planning takes hard work from both partners.

This book gives you a balanced picture on how to reach your financial goals and live to tell about it. You won't read about money just from the scorned woman's perspective. Nor will you read about it from the emotionally starved man's perspective, for that matter. You'll get a balanced view from a husband-wife team that had to fight each other (just a bit) to give you the complete story.

For your benefit, we've taken the jargon out of saving, investing, insurance and estate and retirement planning, and spelled everything out in plain English. We want understanding your finances to be as easy as learning how to pick up a telephone.

Part of gaining control of the family's money is learning who you are and how you relate to your spouse. By making a conscious effort to work though disagreements about money, you really can prosper.

Love, Marriage, and Money can help guide you through important personal and financial decisions in different stages of your life together. It will help you:

- Understand your financial personalities.
- Figure out who should pay for what when you are dating.
- Deal with a wedding.
- Decide whose name to use.
- Decide whether you need a prenuptial agreement.
- Avoid money-related stress.
- Live successfully as a one-wage or two-wage earning couple.
- Share your money.
- Get the right insurance coverage.
- Cooperate on spending, saving, and investing.
- Buy a home and prepare for a child.
- Plan a happy retirement.
- Leave money to your loved ones.

How to Use This Book

This book zeroes in on all the important information you need as a couple to make financial decisions together throughout your lives, starting now. The important details about love, marriage, and money are covered in three parts.

Part One, "We've Got the Love, but Who's Got the Money," explains how to get in sync both financially and in the way you communicate with one another. This section nails down how you handle money when you are dating, making plans for a wedding, and buying a diamond. You also will learn about your financial personality — whether you are a spender or a saver — and what type of investor you are. If you are fortunate enough to have a lot of money, you'll learn if a prenuptial agreement is right for you. You'll also learn about your financial obligations when you marry. Plus, you'll learn how to avoid money-related stress if you are a one-paycheck or two-paycheck couple. Confused about your married name? This part looks into whether a woman should choose to change her name when she weds.

Part Two, "Sprouting a Money Tree," serves up easy-to-use advice about how to share your money. What's the best kind of life, health, and disability insurance you both need. You will learn how to cooperate on a family spending plan. There are tips on how to communicate to one another, so that you don't spend all your time fighting or, worse yet, holding in anger. This part also takes a close look at important financial issues you face during different stages of your life together. Learn what's right for you, such as how you should invest, ways to agree on a happy retirement, and calculating Social Security, other income, and your pension. You will also learn whether you should have a will or a trust—all the important stuff you need to know about estate planning.

Part Three, "Managing Your Money," gets into the nitty-gritty money decisions couples have to make, such as renting or buying a home. You'll also get all the important financial information you need to know about having a baby and those big expenses that come afterward. Although we hope you never get divorced, we've given you information on how to do it. On a happier note, you learn how to enjoy your retirement together and how you can live comfortably. Plus you'll find out some of the best places to retire in America.

Extras

For many of you, money might seem like the most boring of the three subjects of this book. So we're making it easy. Look for these elements to point you in the right direction:

- How to Communicate. Hunt for these sidebars for easy-to-use techniques on how to get your point across—without alienating your partner or the rest of your family.

- Hot Tips. These little tidbits help smooth the road to reaching your goals—whatever they may be.
- Bet You Didn't Know. These sections are designed to provide more information on the subject—or to reveal some juicy nuggets of gossip we uncovered.

Enjoy. We hope that *Love, Marriage, and Money* sends you on the road to both prosperity and marital bliss. Drop us a line at MWliblav@aol.com.

Acknowledgments

We would like to thank the following special people who have helped us and stuck by us through the years.

Special thanks to Cynthia Zigmund, Editorial Director with Dearborn Financial Publishing, for making our book a wonderful reality.

Also, Carol Ann Wilson of Quantum Financial Inc., Boulder, Colorado, for taking her valuable time to comment on our book.

We would also like to express appreciation to our editors at various publications for their support. Robert K. Heady, founder of *Bank Rate Monitor*, who brought us together professionally, leading to, among other things, a happy marriage. Also to the *Boston Herald* for running Alan Lavine's column for 15 years and, more recently, our joint husband-wife column, "Family Finances," on Sundays. Special thanks to Ted Bunker, business editor of the *Boston Herald* and Mary Helen Gillespie, former business editor, who, as our wedding present, placed our first husband-wife column in print. Thanks also to Evan Simonoff, editor of *Financial Planning*; Tom Siedell, managing editor of *Your Money*; John Wasik, senior editor, *Consumers Digest*; Susan Postlewaite, managing editor for the Miami, Ft. Lauderdale, and Palm Beach *Daily Business Review*; Robert Powell, editor-in-chief of *Dalbar Inc.,* Boston; Joe Thoma, editor of *50 Plus Lifestyles*, a publication of Scripps-Howard; Rick Telberg, editor of *Accounting Today*; Pete Phillips, editor of *NAPFA Advisor*; Charles DeRose, host of the "Financial Advisor" syndicated radio program on

United Stations Radio Network; Christy Heady, America Online's MoneyWhiz; and Marla Brill, founder of the Internet's Mutual Funds Interactive: www.brill.com.

For their inspiration and encouragement, we thank Robert Deitchman, Ph.D., at University of Akron, and Avner Arbel, Ph.D., at Cornell University.

We also would like to thank the following experts for their valuable input into the book: Diann Dee Michael, Ft. Lauderdale, Florida-based clinical psychologist and visiting professor at Nova University; Jay Darby, attorney with Sherburne, Powers & Needham P.C.; Roger Smothers, psychotherapist in Friendsville, Pennsylvania, and financial planner in Binghamton, New York; Jane King, Wellesley, Massachusetts-based certified financial planner; Owen Ryan, family therapist from Worcester, Massachusetts, Diana B. Kahn, Coral Gables, Florida-based certified financial planner; Boston attorney Joseph G. Abromovitz; Jeanne Salvatore, director of consumer affairs for the Insurance Information Institute, New York; Jeff Marcus, of Marcus Jewelers, West Palm Beach, Florida; and Alan Pattee of the Alan Pattee Insurance Agency Inc., West Palm Beach, Florida.

We've Got the Love, but Who's Got the Money

This section gets you through the financial repercussions of your relationship and marriage. Like Johnny Appleseed, we hope to plant the seed, at least from the money perspective, for this marriage to be happy enough to last for eternity. You'll learn the art of determining who should pay on a date, how to cut the expenses of going out on the town, and how best to purchase that symbol of everlasting love—no, not money, but a diamond. You'll also learn what marriage really means—financially, that is—and how to survive both the expense and financial stress of your wedding and, finally, your own very special union.

Chapter 1

United We Stand.
Alone We're Broke

Congratulations! We assume if you've reached this stage, you've joined forces in more ways than one. You're happy and either falling in love or you're already there. Unfortunately, apart from all the bliss you're probably experiencing, there are some green paper guys you've got to deal with. In this chapter, we'll tell you how to get those "dollar signs" under control from day one, and hopefully, keep them there once and for all. Knowing the basics about how to handle and talk about your newly combined finances (or even debts, for that matter) can provide a strong foundation for your long term relationship.

Who Pays? What It All Means

In study after study, money has been listed as the number one cause of all marital arguments. It's no wonder. Dollar signs start rearing their ugly heads almost as soon as we begin dating. Take the example of one frustrated man who enjoyed hanging out at the library and art museums—certainly a potentially interesting man to many a young woman. His complaint? Women graded their dates by the amount of money they spent and the types of cars they drove.

All this poor soul wanted was a woman on his wavelength who was unafraid to try new things.

The financially limiting scope of the women this gentleman had been dating, unfortunately, was thwarting his efforts to meet Ms. Right. It also was hindering his dates' own efforts to find the right man, whom, we're sure if they took the time to think about it, merited consideration for some other qualities besides money.

In this common cry that we've heard echoed by many other men, money serves as a turn-off too early on in a relationship. Perhaps this is one reason today's women (and men) are having such difficulties finding mates.

But, we must admit, money also surfaced as a point of stress when we began our relationship. Needless to say, we overcame one money hurdle early on. Although neither of us was exactly making millions, we were enjoying fine conversation and burritos at Pedro's Cantina in Juno Beach, Florida. We both suddenly got a touch of heartburn not triggered by the hot sauce—the bill. Neither of us raced for our wallets. While we wound up splitting the damage reluctantly but equally, these thoughts haunted our relationship:

> *Al:* Most of the women I dated in Boston, where I lived for 15 years, insisted on paying their share of the bill for a night on the town. They refused to let me treat them. Now I'm very confused. I really care about Gail, but based on my past experience, women don't like men to pick up the tab—it's too macho. Besides, business is bad and I'm short on fuel for a while.

> *Gail:* He couldn't really care very much about me. If he had any respect for me, he would have put the whole thing on a credit card.

Fortunately, we subsequently discussed these emotions and understood each other's feelings. It's a good thing. We learned that once you understand how you both think about money you can work things out later on when you get hitched. It doesn't mean there won't be disagreements and spats. But if you can compromise when dating, you can do it after you sign on the dotted line and you can live happily ever after.

All this kind of trouble with money starts early. Since the 1960s, nobody has told us who should pay for what. So how can we make the right move? It used to be easy. Women were considered inferior, so they were treated by the opposite sex with extraordinary politeness. That included having their tabs picked up at all times by men who were exhibiting proper etiquette.

But by the early 1980s, it was clear that women expected to be treated equally to men in the business world. So how does that affect dating?

Colliers Encyclopedia seems to indicate that men stand to score big on a date if they pick up the tab: "In general, older women and younger women who are quite conservative expect the traditional courtesies," says the encyclopedia on the subject of etiquette. "Most women, even those who don't expect these courtesies, will react positively when men go by the old rules."

However, the encyclopedia stresses, "It is now socially acceptable in most circles for a woman to ask a man to go out with her on a date. This new freedom of women has side benefits for men: whoever extends the invitation pays the bill."

Can Money Buy, Ahem, Favors?

There may be another issue to consider in determining who should pay on a date. Date rape has been tossed around as a possible byproduct of who pays.

Sometimes when people are dating, the person who spends most of the money may feel entitled to go farther in terms of sexual intimacy.

For example, teenage boys may want more from their dates than a kiss goodnight at the front door if they pay for Suzie's night on the town. Then again, women at any age may have to be careful if they initiate any spending. If they ask a man out on a date, or, if they offer to share expenses, it easily can be misperceived as wanting you-know-what.

Of course, we also know of many a rejected man whose innocent intention in treating on a date merely was to be polite.

Is your mind, like ours, now totally befuddled on the issue of who really should pay on a date?

No doubt. Money can be a means to an end. However, a lot depends on the type of woman or man you're going out with, and how you relate to each other.

One thing we would like to point out before you consider the controversial issue of who should pay on dates and what it all means, is that money merely is a tool to obtain your goals. It does one of two things in a relationship: It may serve as an area of dispute, or it may serve as an area of agreement. Our goal is to have it serve as a point of agreement. So perhaps placing so much emphasis on your date's financial situation, or who pays for a date, could be a devastating mistake.

The Advantages of Money: Dinner in Palm Beach?

"Money," notes Olivia Mellan in her excellent book *Money Harmony* (Walker and Company, New York), "does not equal happiness, love, power, freedom, selfworth, or security. Money equals dollars and cents."

To prove it does not equal happiness, Mellan suggests that you try keeping track of what you spend your money on for one week or month, and on a scale of 1 to 10, rate the fulfillment that expenditure brings you. You're apt to be surprised that the greatest expenses trigger less fulfillment than smaller expenses.

To prove that money doesn't equal love, ask Todd Powell, an instrument technician from Pace, Florida, who in 1995, at the age of 31, won $27 million in the Florida lottery. His wife, Janet, filed for divorce almost three weeks after his supposed good fortune. Arguments over what to do with the money accelerated their separation, he says. Over two years, he loaned $30,000 to friends he has never seen again, and as of this writing, he was all alone in his dream house on six acres of land.

So perhaps, rather than letting financial conditions or money perceptions rule your quest for a mate, deciding who should pay for a date could be your first major point of agreement on the subject. Or, if one party already has made that decision and the other has a different opinion, talk about your emotions with one another. In fact, a special meeting on the issue of money, perhaps in a park, may be turned into a conveniently low-cost date aimed at getting the relationship off on the right foot.

We started talking at the beginning of our relationship. Fortunately, it worked.

1 / United We Stand. Alone We're Broke

7

HOW TO COMMUNICATE

1. To discuss an issue, express your emotions to your partner. Starting with the words, "I feel_____ because...

2. Be here now. Keep your conversation in the present tense, and help your date express feelings in the present tense. It's too easy to avoid issues when one of you slips into the past or future.

3. Pay close attention to your partner's response, and try to completely understand how he or she feels on the same issue.

4. Communicate to your partner by saying "I understand" and restate what he or she says to confirm that you do.

5. If you can compromise on "it," do so. If not, and you want the relationship to continue, agree to tolerate some aspect of "it," while suggesting that your partner stop the part that really gets on your nerves.

Saving, Yet Living It Up

OK etiquette-wise, at least, the batting average still leans toward men picking up the tab with many women. But regardless of who picks it up, it can be quite a financial blow if you don't have money. This means stress at the onset of a relationship that nobody needs. Here's where a little creativity can help.

We'd like to remind you that you needn't spend a fortune to score points with your date (or spouse, for that matter). For starters, we suggest picking up the Friday entertainment section of your newspaper, which typically lists all the happenings for the week—including free concerts, book fairs, or discounted admissions in the area. Scour it carefully.

Al: Let's go to the PGA tournament.

Gail: Ugh. What about a Saturday movie matinee?

In most areas we've visited, for example, there are free art festivals, flea markets, or inexpensive antique shows—particularly when the weather is warmer. Most movie theaters have lower-price matinees. Often, you can get in cheaper if you go before 5 PM. Shopping center movie theaters have popular flicks on a second run for $2. Then, you may still be able to catch the "pretheater" dinner at a local restaurant, and save about 50 percent off the cost.

Chinese and Thai restaurants tend to be low-cost yet classy and healthy places to dine. Mexican food also is relatively inexpensive.

Research the happy hours in town, where you might be able to find free hors d'oeuvres and half-price drinks. Most local newspapers have a Friday supplement that lists tons of cheap things to do.

A romantic dinner at somebody's home is always another option. Pastas tend to be among the lowest-cost foods to prepare. You can pick up a bottle of red wine for $6 or less.

Here are some other lower-cost ideas that can save you money and still lead to a good time:

- Make a date to go to a book signing. These are free and authors often give stimulating talks.
- Schedule an athletic date. A long walk past the area's mansions, or a Saturday walk in the park.
- It's winter? What about ice skating together?
- If you're going to the theater, schedule a matinee. Off-season, you might be able to locate

> ☞ *Hot Tip* • • •
>
> **H**ave an unusually large amount of money or are you poor as a church mouse? While trying to be honest, refrain in your initial date conversations from sharing such information until you've built trust in other areas of your relationship. As we'll discuss further in Chapter 2, various learned behaviors about money can color your relationship—perhaps unfairly.
>
> • • • • •

low-price shows.

- Check out a comedy club. Often, they have two-for-one admission on off-nights.
- Have a car? Plan a day trip to an area that's within driving distance and has an interesting attraction.
- Visit a museum.
- Buy a discount book or card for going out. The IGT Charge Card (800-444-8872), for example, offers a 25 percent discount at a number of hotels and restaurants.
- Attend a sporting event. Minor league baseball or basketball teams often have low-cost tickets.
- Belong to a health club? Bring your date as a guest. Even if you don't belong, perhaps you can get a one-day pass together.
- Visit the nearest zoo, aquarium, planetarium, or wildlife refuge.
- Look into church, synagogue, or other religious events.
- In warm weather, a picnic by a lake or in a park, a trip to the beach, or a fishing expedition are a few options.
- Meet for espresso at one of the increasing numbers of coffee houses that have been springing up around the country.
- Make a lunch date instead of a dinner date. It's cheaper and, at least initially, may help avoid some of the queasiness triggered by intimacy issues that creep up too early.
- Local universities often have free or low-cost movies, guest lectures, and plays.
- Take a tour together if one is available near you.
- Begin cutting back on your other fixed expenses, so you'll have more money in your pocket, i.e., clip coupons when you shop for food, make certain you're on the lowest-cost telephone and electric company plans, or cut your insurance, so you'll have more money to enjoy dating and to invest.
- Go food shopping together.

Whatever you do, don't run up your credit card bill. Even if you get a good deal by using the card to pay for something, that advantage disappears quickly if you're paying interest on an unpaid balance.

This Is Serious—Making Plans

If you've decided to tie the knot, you've probably reached at least the second major financial hurdle of your relationship: the wedding. It's easy to get caught up in fantasy when you read about weddings like Ivana Trump's to Italian businessman Riccardo Mazzachuelli. For a bride, what can be more glamorous than wearing a suit trimmed with pearls. Can there really be much better entertainment than pianist Peter Duchin and three complete orchestras? How about having, as yes, Ivana did, a one-storey-high wedding cake to grace the affair?

Reality check. Weddings, even those without any of the glitz of Ivana's, can be expensive. For most people, the cost can run anywhere from $8,000 to $50,000. Also, as Ivana has demonstrated, the amount you spend on a wedding doesn't necessarily improve your marriage. Fortunately for women, times have changed. The bride or the bride's family used to foot nearly the entire wedding bill, while the groom or his family covered the honeymoon, bachelor party, and home.

As couples began marrying later in life and women's liberation questioned the toll the expense took on the bride and her family, these customs have eroded. Nevertheless, some families still follow them. Currently, about one-third of all couples pay for their weddings themselves and another one-third follow the traditional route of expecting the bride's family to pay. The remainder use a mix of financing, in which the couple might share expenses with both families. As with dating, who pays for what in the wedding has become a matter you both

Bet You Didn't Know

• • • • •

Considering a trip to the altar? Be absolutely certain you're making the right move—before you're engaged. Break off an engagement and you could open yourself up to a "breach of promise" lawsuit.

Then, of course, there's also the ring. Who keeps it if the big day is called off? While some brides have won the right to keep rings in the wake of broken engagements, the American Bar Association suggests that it be returned. An engagement ring usually is viewed as "a gift given in anticipation of marriage." If the marriage is off, so is the condition of that gift.

• • • • •

need to discuss with each other and your families.

Much depends on the financial situation of everyone, and on religious and personal convictions. It's another financial hurdle for the lovebirds to scale.

We both understand the pleasure of having family and friends of both the bride and groom together for this landmark event. So, for those who opt to go full-throttle, we'd like to offer some survival tips and ways to cut costs.

Prior to scheduling your wedding, though, another money meeting is in order. It's important that both of you know what you own, what you owe, your sources of income, and who will or won't be working after the marriage.

Have one of you had credit problems, such as a bankruptcy? We suggest you fess up before the knot is tied. In fact, it may not be a bad idea to order your individual credit reports and go over them together. It's best to know ahead of time if you're going to be sharing each other's financial headaches. Besides, you'll both certainly want any credit report errors corrected way in advance of buying a home together. Assuming we haven't turned up anything too detrimental to this otherwise wonderful union, proceed with the wedding plans.

Back to your fantasy wedding. Less wealthy couples have successfully

☞ *Hot Tip* • • •

Considering eloping? Don't tell family and friends the good news in the evening. Nobody will be able to sleep that night!

• • • • •

Bet You Didn't Know

• • • • •

It may sound crass, but it pays to consider both of your tax situations in the timing of your wedding plans. Of course, you should check with your accountant (tax laws keep changing), but as of this writing, a couple with two incomes typically paid more in taxes as a married couple than prior to tying the knot. In fact, accountants often refer to this as the "marriage penalty."

If both of you are working and in a high income tax bracket, you may want to consider postponing the marriage at least until after January 1 of the following year.

On the other hand, if just one of you works, marriage could work to your tax advantage. Not only will no income be added to your return, but you get a second personal exemption deduction. Plus, the tax tables treat you better.

• • • • •

used creativity to outsplash the glitz money adds to wedding ceremonies. Take the two runners who stopped in the middle of the New York City Marathon in front of TV cameras, dressed in some pretty unique marriage clothes or remember the weddings that occurred in the snack aisle at a 7-Eleven and in a Harley-Davidson motorcycle shop. Low-cost, perhaps, but definitely equally meaningful and attention-getting alternatives to an Ivana Trump-like event.

It's particularly difficult nowadays to plan for a wedding with two people working, let alone come up with the money to pay for it, and foot the bill for a honeymoon and home. While your wedding most likely will be a major

Bet You Didn't Know • • • •

You might know everyone in the world, but you needn't necessarily invite them all to your wedding. Despite their prominence, John F. Kennedy Jr. and Carolyn Bessette had just 40 guests at theirs.

• • • • •

☞ *Hot Tip* • • •

- To avoid prewedding arguments, let the people who will help foot the wedding bill have a say in how their bucks are spent. This can be frustrating, but remember how much you love your future spouse.
- When a lot of money is being spent, you can count on somebody being offended somehow. Sometimes it's better if you don't get involved. Instead, have somebody in the wedding party who has good communication skills smooth things over. Have the envoy express understanding of the situation but gently remind the angry party that everyone has one common goal: to celebrate the couple of honor. Then, suggest that they all work together to find a solution.
- Don't let the spending get too far out of hand. Blow too much on a wedding and it could haunt you later on. You don't want to get into a spat about money five years down the road because you spent more than you could afford on your wedding day.
- Don't like Aunt Sadie's angel food cake because it sits like rock in your stomach? On your wedding day, it pays to give out warm fuzzies anyway. Or, take a bite and tell her it tastes just like the restaurant downtown. You don't have to say which one.

• • • • •

splurge, you'll make your initial life together a lot easier if you avoid getting into too much debt from it.

By setting the date one to two years away and immediately planning a budget, you and your families will be able to sock away money monthly for some time. It's a good strategy to minimize the amount you must borrow or even get discounts for paying cash. Plus, you'll avoid some of the problems that can occur if you don't plan far enough in advance, such as not being able to rent the spot that you want or needing to have a wedding dress redesigned. Give each party contributing to the affair a portion to finance, complete with the pricetag.

This Fine Day, Please Hire Professionals!

When planning your special day, don't be satisfied with vendors' price estimates. Get everything very specifically described in writing. Make the musicians give you all costs, including a description of what happens if they have to play later than expected. Obtain the written price and description of the silver, china, glassware and serving pieces.

Avoid relying solely on offers by family or friends to take photos of your wedding. Hire a professional, experienced, wedding photographer. This is too important an event to risk missing! Be specific to the photographer about the types of shots you want and who you want photographed. Remember to tell those you want photographed when and where they need to be (we speak from experience on this one). Each person you hire should be interrogated about credentials, length of time in business, number on staff, and number of weddings being handled the week of yours. Shop around.

Close to deciding on a caterer? Ask to visit a wedding reception the caterer is handling to be sure you've made the right choice.

☞ Hot Tip • • •

Considering a gift registry for china? Why not start a registry for the downpayment on a new home instead? Many lenders are offering such a program with no commitment that you get your mortgage from them. To find a lender near you that has such a program, call 1-800-CALL-FHA.

• • • • •

To minimize everyone's financial stress, you might consider delaying your honeymoon until after some of the wedding bills are paid off. Instead, go away immediately after the event for a long, but inexpensive weekend. You also may want to live in one of your existing homes initially so you don't immediately have to finance a house while paying off those wedding bills. More about this idea in Chapter 12.

The wedding industry is big-time, with the average wedding cost running $16,000 to $20,000. But you don't nec-

Bet You Didn't Know

• • • • •

Concerned about being out of vogue if you don't marry in June? Don't be. John Kennedy, Jr. and Carolyn Bessette, as well as Christie Brinkley and Peter Cook, tied the knot on September 21, 1996. Actress Brooke Shields and Andre Agassi married on April 19, 1997.

• • • • •

essarily have to fuel its expansion. One lower-cost idea is to have the wedding at home, with buffet tables and cooked-to-order food. A backyard tent can run $100 to $500.

If you decide to rent a facility, consider avoiding Saturday nights and the month of June. Quieter, and perhaps, lower-cost options in many areas are Friday night and Sunday afternoon, and the months of January and February. Also avoid renting high-priced china.

Daisies, mums, and carnations are cheaper than roses. In fact, it may pay to ask your florist which flowers will be in season. You'll not only be right in style, but you'll save money at the same time. Rental of flowers or fresh fruit in baskets also might help lower costs. Chicken tends to be one of the cheapest foods to serve, in addition to vegetable hors d'oeuvres. Chances are your guests won't mind this lower-calorie and healthier choice. Avoid brand names in liquor that could jack up prices. Also stay clear of unnecessary gimmicks, such as special swizzle sticks. It pays to purchase a bridal gown that the bride will be able to wear again. In fact, you can really save money by shopping at a local thrift or consignment shop for your gown. Chances are any resales only have been worn once. Plus, you might be able to get some pretty stylish castaways if you shop in the ritzy section of town. Cut invitation costs by creating them on a computer and laser printer.

If time rather than money is your concern, you might consider a one-stop bridal shop or a wedding palace that handles everything from the food to the music. You also could consider hiring a wedding planner, which typically charges 10 to 15 percent of the total wedding costs to take on the responsibility. But it is possible to cut your costs and hire a planner, say, on an hourly basis. To locate a wedding planner near you, contact the Association of Bridal Consultants, 200 Chestnutland Road., New Milford, CT 06776 (860-355-0464), or National Bridal Service, 3122 W. Cary St., Richmond, VA 23221 (804-355-6945).

Check with the local Better Business Bureau to make sure there are no unresolved complaints against any of the vendors you plan to use.

If you are taking your honeymoon immediately after the wedding, expect to spend close to $4,000 inside the continental United States and more in Hawaii or Alaska, or outside the United States. Seven to nine days is the typical period for a honeymoon. But 10 to 14 days may be more practical for Hawaii or Europe—places that generally take a long time to get to.

Using a travel agency? Make certain it's a reputable one. Check to see that your travel agent is a member of the American Society of Travel Agents (ASTA). The American Automobile Association and American Express are national agencies known to give good service. To save money, always ask for special packages and consider traveling off-season. In Florida, for example, avoid January, February, and March, and you'll typically pay lower rates. On the other hand, keep in mind that off-season, you also may have the threat of hurricanes or other bad weather, bug season, or closed attractions.

It's possible to purchase trip cancellation insurance, which generally

☞ *Hot Tip* • • •

You can buy wedding-honeymoon insurance, recently expanded and renamed "celebration insurance." For close to $200, at the time of this writing, you could get $500,000 worth of liability coverage plus $3,000 worth of nonrefundable deposit coverage through Fireman's Fund, Novato, California (1-800-ENGAGED). It covers cancellation or postponement of the wedding for reasons out of the insured's control, such as illness, death of one of the couple, job loss, and calls to military duty. However, it won't pay if you or your partner simply has a change of heart.

• • • • •

costs 5 to 7 percent of the cost of the vacation. So a $5,000 trip might cost $250 to $350 to insure. It covers you if the tour operator goes out of business or if you had to cancel the trip due to sickness, a death in the family, or other calamity. If you take this route, make sure you get it from an independent insurance agent rather than the travel agent. Also, always put your trip on a credit card. Many cards automatically provide insurance against bankrupt airlines or other travel headaches.

Buying a (Hiccup) Diamond

One of the most costly outlays for your wedding is the diamond engagement ring. Because it's typically the man who foots the bill out of love for his intended, it can serve as a point of stress if a woman wants a more expensive diamond than the husband can afford. Another issue capable of triggering an Excedrin headache: The husband wishes to give his fiance a more expensive diamond than he can afford. Before beginning your shopping excursion, consider whether you both might need to tone down your expectations in this area to fit your budgets.

Needless to say, prices of diamonds can run from hundreds to thousands of dollars.

☞ *Hot Tip* • • •

Be forewarned. You'll realize your lost independence when you receive checks as wedding gifts. Once your names are joined together with the word "and," both of your signatures will be required to endorse a check, according to the Uniform Commercial Code. It's only when your names are separated by the word "or" that just one of you can endorse it.

• • • • •

☞ *Hot Tip* • • •

Before your honeymoon:

- Call in advance to book a king-size bed and secure your desired room.
- Confirm reservations the day before.
- Set a limit on how much you'll spend.
- Consult a reputable travel agent likely to know about special deals. Check the agent out first with the Better Business Bureau.
- Tell the hotel or resort that it's your honeymoon. You just might qualify for a special deal!

• • • • •

If you're considering a diamond on a limited budget, which most people are, we suggest that you take steps at least to make certain you get the most for your money.

Deal only with reputable dealers, preferably someone a friend has recommended. Check how long the jeweler you are considering has been in business. National trade associations you might examine for your jeweler's membership include the American Gem Society. Other trade groups are the Jewelers of America or the Diamond Council of America.

It's a good idea to tell the jeweler up-front how much you want to spend. Also, bone up on information about diamonds. A reputable jeweler should be able to obtain exactly the grade diamond you're looking for if you ask for it. He or she won't try to talk you into spending more. Try to deal with the manager or assistant manager or the person who typically has the greatest expertise in stones. Most diamonds are purchased in November and December, so you might want to try to avoid doing your shopping during those busy months.

As usual, we advise making major purchases with cash. But if the ring costs a small fortune, use a major credit card. Major card issuers have buyer protection plans.

Watch out for lines of credit or charge cards that boast no interest for a period of time. You could wind up paying rates of at least 20 percent for several months afterward or owe the full amount once the loan comes due. Read all flyspeck type on any borrowing agreements. Also, watch out for financing arrangements—particularly prevalent in chain stores—that will charge more interest than you might otherwise pay because they bank on a certain amount of defaults. Buy a ring for $3,000 and make only the minimum monthly payments on one of these high-rate cards, and you

Bet You Didn't Know

Exactly, how much you should spend on a diamond is a subject for dispute even among experts. As of this writing, the average diamond ranged from $1,200 to $3,000. Financial experts say you should limit the cost of a diamond to three weeks' salary or 6 percent of your annual salary.

Diamond industry spokespeoples, on the other hand suggest you spend two months' salary. Of course, it's easy to see the reason for the disparity since the diamond industry has a stake in increasing sales.

could find yourself paying triple that amount!

When you are buying a diamond, consider—in order—the "4 Cs"—color, clarity, cut, and carat (weight). Ask to look at the diamond under a loupe which is like a magnifying glass. The whiter or clearer the color, the better it is. Look for its grade. "D" means it is absolutely colorless and particularly rare. The worst grade, by contrast, is "Z." Chances are you won't be able to afford a totally colorless diamond, but you need not despair. After all, the Hope diamond is blue, and the Tiffany diamond is canary yellow.

> **☞ Hot Tip • • •**
>
> **B**efore entering a store, check out the lighting. If you see a blue light, hightail it out fast. All gems look great in blue light.
>
> Best to examine your diamond on the counter under a color-balanced fluorescent bulb.
>
> • • • • •

The next important factor in considering a diamond is "clarity." You're looking for a diamond with few spots, bubbles, or lines. You'll always find some of these "inclusions" or natural imperfections. The Gemological Institute of America grades clarity ranging from "FL" or "flawless," in which no blemishes can be seen under a loupe, to "I3" or "imperfect," in which inclusions that can affect the stone's beauty or durability are visible—possibly to the naked eye. But inclusions of foreign bodies often can be camouflaged in the ring's setting, so don't think you're necessarily getting a dud if you see a few.

The quality of a stone's cut is what gives it its sparkle. The facet angles and their proportions constitute the cut. Don't confuse the cut with the shape, which is the outline of the diamond, such as round, pear, oval, emerald, or rectangular.

The fourth important consideration is a diamond's weight. One carat equals .007 ounce and one ounce equals 140 carats. 100 points equals one carat.

"Somebody should buy what we call an "eye-clean stone,'" suggests Jeff Marcus, whose jewelry store, Marcus Jewelers, has been in business in West Palm Beach, Florida, for 20 years. "That means that looking at the stone without a loupe, from the top of the stone, you do not see the inclusions. The next thing is you'd want the stone to be white—not off-color. If you've got a white,

1 / United We Stand. Alone We're Broke

19

eye-clean stone, you at least have a pretty stone. From that point on, it depends on your pocketbook."

Buy your diamond at chain stores in a mall and you'll probably pay more, Marcus warns. Plus, you're more apt to get salespersons rather than knowledgeable jewelers.

Unfortunately, Marcus says, it's possible to get a good price on a stone that you want and still good hoodwinked simply by not getting all the information. Marcus cites the client who was able to track down a great deal on exactly the type of stone he wanted, but it was a "dead" stone. "It looks like cubic zirconia," Marcus explains. "There is no dispersion of light or color." Even though diamonds might meet your demands for an impressive grade, he says, a certain number of stones, based on the way they are formed in the ground, wind up dead. "There are a lot of these around," he says.

> **Bet You Didn't Know**
> • • • • •
>
>
> **A** diamond's color can be improved by radiation treatment, so it's always best to get a written statement from your dealer that the color is natural.
> • • • • •

> **☞ Hot Tip** • • •
>
> **A**n ideally cut diamond can cost up to 50 percent more than one with several imperfections—even though both weigh the same.
> • • • • •

While the world gives much emphasis to the "carat" or weight of the diamond, Marcus adds, a stone with an impressive weight may not necessarily be nicely proportioned—a point that also can hurt its value.

Marcus suggests getting a guarantee from a jeweler who appraises and grades the stone. The guarantee should consist of an offer to buy it back "so that there's no question they're telling the truth."

Above all, both of you should make certain you're happy with your purchase. While many a movie and song would have us think that you're wealthy if you own a diamond, they rarely appreciate as much as most people think. So you want to really like it.

Getting in Sync

Have you ever tried carrying a big heavy suitcase to your car and then forgotten where you were parked? We're willing to bet that the heavy tugging on your arm is nothing compared with the emotional baggage you've been carrying around on the subject of money. Unfortunately, too many people don't realize this before they tie the knot. We're sure many of you have some unbridled energy when it comes to spending money (or saving it, for that matter). Much of this is not your fault. Virtually all of us have heavy emotional ways of dealing with dollar bills that may have started years ago with our parents. This chapter is designed to help you understand your attitudes about money and how they are affecting your relationship. It is only when the two of you figure out what is influencing your behaviors on the subject of money that you can avoid some of those spats for which neither of you really is to blame.

Understanding Your Financial Personalities

Money problems, although they seem to create the most stress and friction in a marriage, don't always stem from not having enough—although the lack of money triggers many arguments.

Friction also can arise if money leads to unbalanced behavior, or if certain personality traits around money lead to arguments.

The late Lucille Ball, in her book Love Lucy (G.P. Putnam & Sons, New York) said she spotted at least one money conflict with Desi Arnaz right away—even before she married him. "I'm a careful spender," Lucy wrote. "Desi is highly extravagant. It would save a lot of arguments if we kept our incomes and obligations completely separate.

"So right from the beginning of our marriage, our business manager, Andrew Hickox, handled our affairs on this basis."

Each paid personal expenses and contributed a fixed amount every week toward home expenses. Lucy's manager gave each $25 a week for incidentals, and everything else was charged. Checks and bills were paid by their agent from separate accounts.

Even if yours is among the one out of ten marriages that consider money management a strong suit, you're not out of the woods when it comes to money problems. Reason: If you're overly aware about money, you might not communicate well on other matters, or you could lack intimacy.

You might think you have a balanced marriage. But if that's the case, you may fall apart if you don't have enough money, or if you need to discuss it.

So how can you win at this money game and keep alive the love you've finally won?

The first step is to recognize and understand your money personalities. For example, some people go out and spend money when they get upset. Others feel sick when they spend the money. Might you expect Sir or Madam Lancelot to ride in on a white horse and pay off your credit cards? Some people always pick up the tab because they want to be liked.

Don't despair. Even if you've detected a money-triggered bad habit of your own, there's plenty of hope for your marriage. In fact, none of these may be a major problem unless it affects your relationship.

Who's the Spender? Who's the Saver?

Are you a spender or a saver?

Based on our experience and the letters we've gotten from our syndicated column, there are tons of things that can cause fights in a marriage. But when it comes to money, these two personality traits seem to be the most basic of all.

The bottom line, as we see it, is that each of us has his or her own money personality, which, if unchecked, can create conflicts. Bring two people with money problems together, and you have double money troubles. Even if just one person in a relationship has a money problem, conflicts can result. That's why it's important to understand your attitudes about money, and settle any conflicts. Then work together toward your joint financial goals.

Let's face it, in our marriage, it's pretty clear-cut. There definitely is one spender and one saver.

> *Gail (spender):* I like luxury, shopping, having friends over, and inviting people out to dinner.

> *Alan (saver):* I like eating at home, investing, a quiet day alone on the sofa, and golf. No stores, please.

We've been lucky enough to work through these personality differences through many a compromise. Unfortunately, or fortunately, a good part of these behaviors are not our fault. They stem from our past experiences. Take the parents of the spender in our marriage. Both worked for someone else for a living. They, too, enjoyed spending their money on family and friends.

The "thrifty" half of this couple also got much of his behavior from his parents, who owned a produce business and always worried that an economic downturn could affect their income. They were careful to save every penny.

While these behaviors, passed on from one generation to another, may be a source of many a dispute between us, they are not necessarily our fault. Nor is a marriage of a spender with a saver the only potential source of conflict. Two spenders could wind up building up the household debt, and putting stress on a marriage. On the other hand, two penny pinchers could reinforce each other's spartan ways and each could wind up blaming the other for not being able to relax and enjoy life. We're certain that many a psychologist could elaborate on these combinations and others.

Believe it or not, your attitude toward money also may tell a lot about the way you love. Often, a family that is generous with money also is generous with love.

Meanwhile, the penny pincher who is reluctant to part with his or her money may have a hard time showing love, adding other obstacles to a relationship.

Complicating the money patterns each of us already at least partially has obtained from parents are cultural traditions. Many of these traditions are outdated, and place too heavy a burden on either or both sexes. If both of you treat money with equal respect and understanding, you'd actually have a stronger and more prosperous relationship.

> **☞ Hot Tip • • •**
>
> "If you're the saver in the family, remember," says financial planner Jonathan Pond, "misers may be tough to live with, but they make great ancestors."
>
> • • • • •

Women: Are you turned off toward a man who doesn't have much money? This stems from the cultural belief that a man who loves a woman must take care of her, which too often means making a lot of money. This can put a lot of pressure on a man. Some men, we suspect, live in fear that they won't be able to support their families. In fact, many who got laid off in the last recession were devastated because they weren't able to do what was expected of them.

Men: Do you consider your woman incapable of managing money? If so, this is an insecurity that can be brought on by another cultural belief that has been carried on for way too long. Unfortunately, women who buy into this stereotype don't bother to learn how to invest. Meanwhile, this puts another major stress—the family's investment burden—squarely on the man's shoulders.

Women who believe this myth wind up being less successful financially. Not only are they still paid less than men, but some live in fear of losing the little they have. Men who are unwilling to share financial decision-making find themselves carrying an awful lot of financial responsibility they might not always be up to handling.

"The problem is a woman wakes up one day to find out the retirement money she assumed was there is much less than she projected it to be," says Roger Smothers, a financial planner who also runs a psychotherapy practice in

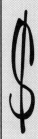

EXERCISE
TO CURB SPENDING
• • • • •

Are you a spender who has gone a bit overboard? Here are some steps you can take to get things under control.

1. Identify activities—apart from spending money—that make you happy. Some ideas: exercise, art, hobbies, relaxation techniques, support groups, discussions, and sports.

2. Make a list of what provokes your overspending. Avoid those triggers. Example: Feel you must stop every time you walk by a certain store on the way home? Take a different route.

3. Spend one week writing down all your purchases. At the end of the week, determine which purchases you really didn't need.

4. Brainstorm ways to cut down on those purchases you didn't need. If you like going out to dinner, for example, avoid the restaurants that cost $100 a person and resolve to go to restaurants that cost $20 each instead.

5. Write down what you really do need, i.e., money for a house or retirement.

6. Determine a specific amount you will deposit into a savings account each week toward those important goals. Make it your priority—before you do anything else with your paycheck.

• • • • •

Binghamton, New York. "On the other hand," he says, "a man who loses a job, for example, is likely to be under particularly heavy strain given the power he feels he needs to have."

"If he loses his job in a corporate setting, and his spouse is beating him up, it's hard enough to get back out there when he feels defeated," Smothers says.

There are some pretty big differences in how men and women view financial decisions too, notes psychotherapist-consultant Olivia Mellan.

- Men tend to take credit when they make money, but blame others if they lose it.
- Women credit others when they make money, but blame themselves when they lose it.
- In fights about money, the man blames the woman while the woman blames herself, but then may resent the man.
- Men tend to be uncomfortable discussing investment decisions with spouses.
- Women almost always go to spouses with financial issues.
- Women feel they need to discuss and plan financial moves more than men do.

Look at your own relationship and those around you. Men typically take more risks. Although they probably won't admit it, they hurt pretty bad when they lose.

Women stick to safer investments. As a result, they lose less. But too frequently, they're afraid to take the risks necessary to make more money long-term.

Meanwhile, put some of these issues into a relationship, and there sure are a lot of reasons for couples to fight!

While spenders can get the family into trouble with debt, savers don't necessarily have to cause problems—unless they happen to hook up with a partner who likes to spend, notes Diann Dee Michael, Ph.D., a Fort Lauderdale, Florida-based psychologist.

"Misers have to realize they're in a world with other people," she says.

Once they do, she says, a miser can learn to relax about spending money if it makes a partner happy. By the same token, she says, a spender who knows he or she has hooked up with a miser, should defer to the miser now and then. Even if the spender would prefer a filet mignon dinner, pancakes can be tolerable when love is involved.

Besides, when you offer to do what your partner wants, whether it comes to spending or saving money, you'd be surprised how much more smoothly your relationship works.

What Type of Investor Are You? Take This Quiz

Well, until now, you might not have realized the impact that your thoughts about money could have on your personal relationship or marriage. However, apart from the personal issue, there are investing issues to consider.

Al: Your growth stock fund is up 25 percent this year!

Gail: Hmmm. Mysterious silence about the rest of our investments.

We mentioned earlier that women tend to be less comfortable taking investment risks—a factor that hurts their ability to earn more money long-term. Men, on the other hand, are more inclined to take risks—sometimes without completely understanding the risks they are taking. Then when they lose, they suffer terrible depressions.

Nevertheless, history has proven that people willing to take some risks and invest in stocks or stock mutual funds for a term of at least 10 or 20 years tend to make more money than more timid investors. The trick—for both men and women alike—is knowing when and how to take such risks.

Take Sam and Henrietta, who are 65 and living on Sam's retirement savings—about $25,000. Sam put the bulk of that money in a stock mutual fund. Two months later, there was a stock market correction and Sam lost $5,000—just after he managed to break a tooth while eating some southern fried chicken. Of course, Sam had no dental insurance and had to cash money out of his fund to pay for a bridge at exactly the wrong time.

Not only did Sam take a big risk with his lifetime savings, but he lost money at exactly the wrong time. Needless to say, his wife Henrietta was very upset, and wouldn't talk to him for a week.

On the other hand, James, a 35-year-old doctor, makes $100,000 a year. He and his wife, Susan, were very comfortable putting $10,000 in the very same stock mutual fund that Sam and Henrietta invested in because they have at least 30 years to retirement. James and Susan both know they don't need the money immediately. So it doesn't matter if the investment is worth only $8,000 after the first year. They know that by the time they retire, based on the stock

---

Figure 2.1 • • • • •

Risk Tolerance Quiz

To determine your risk tolerance, circle the letter that best expresses your answer to the following questions:

1. How old are you?
   a. Over age 65 (1)
   b. Between age 55 and 65 (2)
   c. Between age 35 and 55 (3)
   d. Under age 35 (4)

2. How much are you willing to lose in mutual fund investments in any given year?
   a. 1 percent (1)
   b. 3 percent (2)
   c. 10 percent (3)
   d. 15 percent (4)

3. How important is regular income from your investments to cover expenses now?
   a. Very important (1)
   b. Important (2)
   c. Somewhat important (3)
   d. Not important (4)

4. How important is it to have regular income from your investments to reinvest?
   a. Not important (1)
   b. Somewhat important (2)
   c. Important (3)
   d. Very important (4)

5. How important is it to avoid losses and know your money is safe?
   a. Very important (1)
   b. Important (2)
   c. Somewhat important (3)
   d. Not important (4)

6. How important is it that your money grow faster than the prices you pay for the things you need?
   a. Not as important as getting regular income (1)
   b. I want it to grow as fast as the cost of things I need (2)
   c. I want it to grow more than the cost of things (3)
   d. I want it to grow much faster than the cost of things (4)

Figure
2.1

• • • • •
Risk Tolerance Quiz (cont.)

Now add up the numbers in parentheses to the right of each of your answers to determine
your total risk tolerance score.

- If your score is 10 or less, you are a conservative investor. This means safety is as important
  as seeing your money grow in value over the years. Consider a mix on the order of 40 percent stocks or stock mutual funds, 40 percent in bonds or bond mutual funds and 20
  percent money funds, savings accounts, CDs, or U.S. Treasury securities.
- If you score between 10 and 20, you are a moderate investor. You are willing to see a short-
  term decline in the value of your investment in exchange for long-term growth. Benchmark
  investment mix: 60 percent in stocks or stock mutual funds and 40 percent in bonds or
  bond mutual funds.
- If you score 20 or more, you are an aggressive investor. You are willing to accept larger
  short-term losses in return for substantial gains long-term. Benchmark mix: 80 percent in
  stocks or stock mutual funds and 20 percent in bonds or bond mutual funds.

market average of 10 percent annually, it's likely to grow to $174,494. That's
more than it would likely earn in a CD, which historically has averaged just
about 3 percent over the years.

The trick to investing is understanding your investment and balancing its
risk with the amount of risk you can tolerate. You also need to remember that
keeping all your money in CDs or savings accounts, while not as risky as the
stock market, also presents a risk of its own. That risk is your money may not
grow fast enough to keep pace with inflation, or the price increases in your
everyday living expenses.

How to Compromise: A Handy Checklist

All right. None of us is perfect. Even if you fully understand money and
investing, as well as how you think about money, you're bound to have some

money disputes. So once you've corrected your own bad money habits, you'll probably still need to compromise with each other on money issues.

There are a couple of preliminary rules to follow to reach this goal. First things first. Turn off the television and unplug the telephone, please. Round up all your financial paperwork. Trying to decide on a mortgage? Get the terms of your mortgage agreement or the good faith estimates of the lenders you are considering before either of you opens your mouth.

If you're having a money conflict, keep in mind basic differences between men and women. Men don't like to be told how to act. So women need to make a particular effort to provide positive reinforcement when they communicate. "Honey, I love you, but don't you think it would be in our best joint interests to see a financial planner?" might be one positive way to state your case rather than, "You don't know what you're doing. You already lost us $10,000 last year."

! How to Communicate

Looking to compromise on a money matter without a full-fledged fight?

- Only one person may talk at a time.
- State exactly what you want—clearly.
- Listen carefully to the response.
- Repeat back what you think you heard your spouse or lover say.
- No name-calling.
- Make your points by using the words "I feel" and "I need," rather than putting down your partner.
- Say what you agree with.
- Say what you disagree with.
- Take turns figuring out ways to compromise.

On the other hand, women need more time to analyze and plan things. Men need to respect this. Don't throw the checking statement at her when she's just come home from a day of mind-boggling deadlines at work.

Once you have these basics down, you're apt to eliminate some areas of major conflict.

Chapter 3

"Can't Buy Me Love": Contracts Made in Heaven or Hell

Prenuptial Agreements and Postnuptial Agreements

As lawsuits become a way of life, agreements that spell out conditions to a marriage, death, or divorce, are growing like wildfire. But do these documents generate more conflicts than they resolve? Should you sign them before you tie the knot or afterward? Or ever? Does making decisions in case you break up become a self-fulfilling prophecy? This chapter goes into the pros and cons of prenuptial and postnuptial agreements, both emotionally and legally. It spells out how to bring up the subject of considering an agreement, when such agreements should be signed, and when they should be ignored.

Pros and Cons

John F. Kennedy Jr. and Carolyn Bessette had a low-key wedding in 1996, choosing to exchange vows in front of just 40 people. But the wedding, while modest, was not without a prenuptial agreement, which published reports indicated was designed to protect Kennedy from community property laws in California, where they planned to reside.

The Kennedys' prenuptial agreement was drawn up 12 days before their wedding. Kennedy, worth $32.7 million, would grant Bessette a minimum of $1 million if they divorce after less than three years. However, that figure increases the longer she's married, peaking at $3 million after ten years.

The Kennedys joined an increasing number of couples who are signing on the dotted line before the wedding ceremony. When you get married, state laws entitle you to certain rights. For example, states typically give spouses rights to inherit a certain amount of property—a minimum of one-third in most. Most states generally protect spouses in the event of a divorce. For example, you may get to keep a certain amount of assets, and you may get money to live on, or "alimony." With a prenuptial (also known as an antenuptial) agreement, you actually may be overriding such state laws.

Might such agreements, which spell out the legal rights of each party, actually create more problems than they're worth?

We asked that question of several professionals with years of experience dealing with this gut-wrenching stuff. People like Ronald Sales, a West Palm Beach-based celebrity divorce lawyer who has represented Connie Stevens and Roxanne Pulitizer.

Some argue that prenuptial agreements can create suspicion, reveal a lack of commitment from the start of a marriage, or signal a mate's reluctance to share. All bad stuff when it comes to starting a marriage.

"I can't think it has a positive emotional experience on a marriage," Sales says. The spouse-to-be who has less money or property than the other, he contends, never does as well as the law allows. Otherwise, why would there be such an agreement to begin with?

"The point is," he claims, "they're always unfair!"

It's true that by signing a prenuptial agreement, you may be giving up some rights that as a spouse you otherwise would be entitled to in your state. For example, by signing a prenuptial agreement, one spouse might lose financial support and have to move out of the house in the event of a divorce.

There are no consistent rules to this either. Prenuptial agreements are governed by state laws, which can vary greatly.

Although you may be giving up certain rights by signing a prenuptial agreement, there are certain rights that supersede a prenuptial agreement.

For example, an agreement can't violate a child's right to support.

But prenups can be a tough pill to swallow. People can take them the wrong way. Below the surface, the intended spouse may get the feeling that his or her partner thinks more of money than him or her.

Are prenups any good at all? Fortunately, unless one spouse has substantially more money than the other, or it's a second marriage and you want to be sure your children inherit what's due to them, prenuputials may not be necessary.

> ☞ *Hot Tip* • • •
>
> **C**onsidering a prenuptial agreement? You might talk to an insurance agent. Sometimes life insurance can offer another option to prenuptial agreements.
>
> • • • • •

Nevertheless, the experience of Rex and Teresa LeGalley, married engineers from Albuquerque, New Mexico, appear to have flown in the face of all these arguments against prenuptial agreements. Their 16-page document, filed in the summer of 1995 as a public record at the Bernalillo county clerk's office, deals with much more than the splitting up of property and assets. It stipulated that the couple agreed to engage in healthy sex three to five times per week; they were to retire at 11:30 PM and awake at 6:30 AM; and to live within a budget and "pay cash for everything unless agreed to otherwise."

Also part of the pact was a firm monthly budget and an agreement to leave "nothing. . .on the floor overnight unless packing for a trip."

Both spouses had been married before. Rex said he was eager to avoid mistakes since his two prior marriages had failed, and Teresa, also married once before, thought a written agreement would help both partners take issues seriously.

The couple, at least as of this writing, remain married.

Some lawyers specifically recommend prenuptial agreements for couples with at least $500,000 in assets. They're particularly important if at least one spouse is remarrying and wants to leave something to children from a prior marriage.

So, should you consider a prenuptial agreement?

Some experts argue that too often when the wealthier mate is the woman, a prenuptial agreement is wrongly shunned out of fear that a mate might feel like a "kept man." On the positive side, prenuptial agreements may help reinforce a will, which easily can be contested. In fact, a prenuptial agreement may be easier to enforce than a will because it is signed by both parties. A will is just signed by one. Prenuptial agreements also can cut down on legal fees if—dare we say it—there is a divorce, and make both parties less hostile through that process.

Let's Make a Deal

Here are some situations that might merit discussion of a prenuptial agreement:

- One of you has a lot more money or property than the other.
- It's a second marriage and one or both of you wants to be sure your children from a prior marriage will be taken care of.
- You live in a community property state. In that case, any property a spouse acquires during a marriage is the property of both spouses equally. Community property states are: Arizona, California, Louisiana, Idaho, Nevada, New Mexico, Texas, Washington, and Wisconsin, as well as the territory of Puerto Rico.
- One of you is giving up a paycheck.

Later, Please. . .

Already married? Postnuptial agreements, which spell out legal rights after a couple already has tied the knot, have some of the same purposes as prenuptial agreements. Or, they may be a way to update or renegotiate an existing prenuptial agreement. In some cases, it may resolve serious differences that have arisen.

If you are thinking about a postnup, consult an attorney. "The disclosure requirements are the same, but in the postnuptial agreement, spouses have rights

Bet You Didn't Know
• • • • •

There are four main reasons courts have invalidated prenuptial agreements:
1. Fraud.
2. Failure to fully disclose all assets.
3. Failure of spouses to have separate legal representation.
4. Signing the agreement under physical duress.

• • • • •

to property and have rights to receive spousal support," attorney Sales notes. "In a prenuptial agreement, they have no rights."

The courts, as of this writing, are tending to overturn postnuptial agreements more readily than prenuptial agreements. This is due to courts' concerns that a spouse, who already may be totally dependent on a mate, is less free to reject the agreement.

Bringing Up the "P" Word

OK. One of you has decided you do want a prenuptial agreement or postnuptial agreement, but how can you possibly bring up the subject without raising your spouse's suspicions?

We suggest that you ignore the advice of the late Roy Cohn, who drafted one of three agreements signed by Donald and Ivana Trump. After all, look what happened to their marriage! Cohn advocated white lies like, "I trust you completely, but my family won't allow it."

Other lawyers might suggest that you put the blame on the lawyer. By taking either of these approaches, you're skirting an important area of communication that could hurt your marriage later on.

It's human nature for somebody being approached about a prenuptial agreement to think the person expects a divorce. So handle the subject gently.

Saying something like, "I've really thought about this. I see this as positive to the relationship. Let's get this worked out so we have a sense of clarity about it," suggests our friend, Smothers, a Friendsville, Pennsylvania psychologist-therapist and Binghamton, New York financial planner.

Others say to address the issue right away—extremely early on in the relationship—because it's like banging your head against a brick wall: It feels better when you stop. The last thing you want is to have it come as a complete surprise. That's when there's trouble.

Ft. Lauderdale, Florida psychologist, Diann Dee Michael summed it up best when she told us: "In my experience and all the instances I've seen, the spouse is relieved once a prenuptial agreement is arranged that the spouse is comfortable with."

HOW TO COMMUNICATE

To open the discussion:

1. Discuss your feelings about money.

2. Review the issues that have led to your feelings.

3. Make it clear how much you love your partner.

4. Be businesslike at all times in drawing up the agreement.

5. Obtain legal representation for each partner.

6. Make certain you both consider the agreement fair.

After all, it's perfectly logical to want a prenuptial agreement if one partner is concerned about caring for children from a previous marriage. Meanwhile, it also guarantees money to the other party in the relationship.

How to Set One Up

If you're setting up a prenuptial agreement, once again, it should be prepared well in advance of the signing.

The first step is to make a list of all your assets including everything you bring into a marriage. That can be the toughest part because most people don't necessarily have all their assets on one sheet.

Jane King, CFP, a Wellesley, Massachusetts–based financial planner who's been working with couples and families for more than 25 years, can't over emphasize the importance of organization. "The details can trip you up," she stresses. Many lawyers who have successfully challenged these agreements have challenged them on the basis of items that someone failed to completely disclose.

Among the items that require disclosure are:

- Assets: amounts, locations, and account numbers
- Income
- Inheritance, pensions, retirement plans
- Anticipated future income
- Life insurance and the beneficiaries
- Heirlooms
- Financial institutions and people who handle the money
- Alimony

Real estate and jewelry should be professionally appraised.

Once you've detailed all your assets, make certain your lawyer sets conditions under which the agreement may be renegotiated.

It also should be notarized.

> **Bet You Didn't Know** • • • • •
>
>
>
> **P**ublished reports indicate that Donald Trump and Marla Maples signed a prenuptial agreement before they married in 1993, and as of 1997, have updated it at least once.
>
> • • • • •

Mistakes People Make

While some have called director-producer Steven Spielberg a creative genius, he may have carried his creativity a bit too far. Before marrying actress Amy Irving, he handwrote a prenuptial agreement on a piece of paper—without consulting a lawyer. He and Irving signed it. Fatal mistake. The courts awarded Irving one of the largest divorce settlements in Hollywood, believed to be $100 million.

Spielberg made one of the classic mistakes in negotiating a prenuptial agreement—not having legal representation either for himself or his intended.

Tim Peters, former husband of media heiress Sallie Bingham, made yet another error. He waived all claims to alimony in a prenuptial agreement. Although Peters tried to change the terms later on after they divorced in 1990, the courts ruled against him.

Although these cases represented major notable errors in the area of prenuptial agreements, the law is not always clear-cut. A Massachusetts court upheld a similar situation to the Spielberg prenuptial agreement. In that case, the heiress's annual salary was $540,000 and the agreement was signed three hours before the wedding.

To prove fairness, some lawyers suggest that the wealthier spouse offer a gift at least equal to the share the state mandates, which typically is one-third of the estate. Transferring the assets after the marriage avoids gift tax.

Discuss whether you might need a prenuptial agreement early on in the relationship. Make sure your spouse understands and accepts it without reservations as part of the marriage. Otherwise, it could hurt later on.

Bet You Didn't Know
• • • • •

Jackie Onassis was said to have successfully reopened negotiations of her prenuptial agreement upon the death of her husband, Aristotle, and received more than the original contract stipulated.

• • • • •

Chapter 4

Tying the Knot: Dollars and Sense

All right. You love each other. But is it really to your benefit to marry? Strange question about an institution that was founded on the basis of love. With marriage also comes a lot of legal and financial responsibilities that you need to consider, discuss, and resolve. This chapter nails down the financial and legal issues on marriage as well as some of the emotional ones. It compares marriage with living together, and tells how to pave the way for a successful union—at least from a financial perspective, regardless of which lifestyle you choose. It also seeks to dispel some of the financially related myths that have prevented many an in-love couple from tying the knot.

Marriage: Your Legal and Financial Obligations

To marry or not to marry is not only a matter of love. It also is a matter of—yuck—law and money. Before you determine whether to live together or tie the knot, you first need to know some fairly unromantic aspects of your union as governed by the laws of your state. Unfortunately, too many people don't. Believe it or not, fornication and cohabitation remain illegal in certain places, although such laws are not routinely enforced.

"Goin' to the Chapel and We're Gonna Get Married"

You don't need to be married to be in love and spend money, that's for sure. Most people who do live together get hitched eventually. Evidently, they like it so much they want to make it legal. Either that or their parents and friends get on their cases and show them no mercy.

State laws have not posed a major obstacle against living together out of wedlock. It's been estimated that almost 4 million households have people shacking up compared with some 52 million homes with married couples. Our best guess is that about half of those shacking up will tie the knot.

Bet You Didn't Know

FYI, according to the Living Together Kit (Nolo Press Berkeley, California) fornication is illegal in Georgia, Massachusetts, Mississippi, North Carolina, Idaho, Rhode Island, South Carolina, Utah, and Virginia. Cohabitation is illegal in: Arizona, Florida, Idaho, Michigan, Mississippi, New Mexico, North Carolina, and Virginia.

Getting Married Is Healthier

With marriage comes financial and legal obligations, true. But it also can add some other qualities to an otherwise mundane existence—like romance and a certain stabilizing influence on the human soul.

Our psychologist friends can't emphasize enough the importance of commitments. Don't make it legal and you are asking for trouble. Marriage is a bond that leads to a deep level of love and trust.

Contrary to popular belief, most research indicates that living together first does not necessarily improve your chances of staying together permanently.

Living together does not necessarily make people happier either. There is increasing evidence that both women and men live longer and enjoy better health when married.

We're both happy we got married for many reasons.

Al: Marriage is great—particularly since research indicates that married men tend to live longer than single men and divorced men are twice as likely to die early from hypertension, four times as likely to die early from throat cancer, and seven times as likely to kick the bucket prematurely from pneumonia. If only Gail wouldn't shrink my pants!

Gail: So far, I agree with the research that indicates women who live out of wedlock tend to be more depressed than women who wed. Plus, I married a great—albeit messy—cook.

Sometimes the Pocketbook Tells the Tale

Apart from having your arm twisted on the subject of marriage by state laws, mental and physical health researchers, and our very own admitted bias in favor of the subject, money can and should be an influence. In fact, for many, it is the number one influence.

What do the family therapists have to say about it?

"Money is one thing, and love is another," stresses Florida psychologist Diann Dee Michael. "When we love somebody, it has to do with the movies and music. But marriage is actually a financial and social institution. It's not love. Love exists without marriage."

Michael warns that it's critical not to confuse the religious aspect of marriage with the civil part of it. "To have and to hold from this day forward has nothing to do with a civil marriage," Michael says. "In effect, those are emotional words, and we need to be more practical about other parts of our lives. It makes love grow to be honest about the difference."

Money seems to enter into the picture regardless of whether you marry or live together. In fact, sometimes it drives that decision.

We have a friend, for example, who is living with his fiance before their wedding. "It costs me nothing extra," he says. "Meanwhile, she'll be able to pay off her credit card bills before we get married. I've been married before, and I don't want to go into this marriage with any debt."

This man is not alone. In fact, many senior citizen couples also are forgoing marriage entirely to avoid having their assets tapped for a partner's nursing home or health care costs. In many states, nursing homes or medical institutions can claim a certain amount of assets of both spouses if a couple is married. Not so if the couple is unmarried.

You'll see a lot of seniors living out of wedlock for another good reason—they may be paying more taxes on Social Security if they're married than if they're not. (Other Social Security issues will be discussed later in this chapter.)

On the other hand, if you're not married, your live-in may be unable to decide your care if you become incapacitated and have failed to appoint that person in writing as your health medical care agent or proxy.

Also, if you're living together and not married, it's harder to legally claim some of the benefits typically available to married couples. As you recall from earlier chapters, these benefits typically include:

- You automatically inherit a share of money, property, and other valuable things when your spouse dies.
- You get to keep a certain amount of assets if you get divorced.
- You may get money to live on, or "alimony" if you get divorced.
- In states with "homestead" laws, you have the right to stay in the family home if you get divorced.

Debt also may be a consideration in your decision to get married. If you're married, each spouse has no liability for debts brought into a marriage, but they both are responsible for debts they've cosigned together after they've married.

If you're considering bankruptcy, lawyers tell us you're better off married from the standpoint of debtors' relief. Often, a married person still is entitled to own property in joint names, which would be exempt from creditors' claims.

> **☞ Hot Tip • • •**
>
> **W**orried that your new spouse's ex might try to collect a debt such as alimony or child support? It's best, in that case, not to hold joint property, indicates the American Bar Association Guide to Family Law (Times Books).
>
> • • • • •

Seniors Living Together

As we mentioned earlier, seniors are one particular group that sees benefits to staying single. Yet another motivator for this trend is some are afraid they will lose Social Security benefits or pension benefits if they remarry. Not so—in many cases.

Here's the straight scoop direct from the Social Security Administration: Yes, you may lose Social Security benefits if you've divorced, are receiving benefits based on your ex-spouse's work record, and remarry while he or she is alive.

You also have to worry if you're younger than 60, and you remarry after your spouse dies. You could lose Social Security benefits based on your deceased spouse's work record. By contrast, if you're at least 60 years old when you remarry, you still can collect based on your deceased spouse's record. And once you become 62, you have the option to collect benefits based on the work record of your former spouse or your new spouse—whichever winds up being greater. These same rules apply if you're divorced and your ex dies—provided that you had been married at least 10 years.

Keep in mind that you still may be able to collect on a former spouse's record if your new marriage ends. Plus, if you're at least 62 you may be eligible based on your own work record.

No need to worry about your company pension. Your monthly checks keep coming when you remarry.

Military plans may suspend pension survivor benefits if surviving spouses marry before age 55. That's pretty crummy. At 55 you're still a young whipper-snapper.

The Bottom Line on Marriage

If you do decide to tie the knot, call the marriage license bureau or clerk of courts in your area to get the rules. State by state, laws differ. You might have to get a blood test or get some shots to protect you against certain diseases. After all, you don't want to get married and come down with yellow fever, right?

> **☞ Hot Tip** • • •
>
> **Q**uestions about Social Security benefits? You can contact the Social Security Administration directly by calling 1-800-772-1213 or going to its Web site at www.ssa.gov.
>
> • • • • •

You might need witnesses for the ceremony, and be sure a copy of the marriage certificate is sent to the department that records marriages.

If you're a woman, you'll need to evaluate whether you want to assume your husband's name. Or, if you're a man, you might wish to consider assuming your wife's name. Yes, it has been done! More about how to change your name in Chapter 6.

Getting a Fair Shake When You Shack Up

> ### Bet You Didn't Know
>
> **A** marriage may be invalidated if one of you is underage or already married. You also can't be related. Plus, if you got married while you were drunk or couldn't think straight, your marriage could be struck down.

If you're living together and hope to obtain some of the benefits married people are entitled to, it's probably more difficult than you think. Contrary to popular belief, only 13 states recognize "common-law marriages," which treat you as if you've had the ceremony if you show you intend to be treated as a married couple and you hold yourself out to the community as married.

If you're shacking up and don't live in the following states, think about moving. You may get a better deal if you live in states that do recognize common-law marriages. The states include: Alabama, Colorado, Idaho, Iowa, Kansas, Montana, Ohio, Oklahoma, Pennsylvania, Rhode Island, South Carolina, Texas, and Utah.

Meanwhile, though, if you have a common-law marriage in a state that recognizes them and you move, you'll be pleased to know that most states will consider you officially married.

State laws differ. So before you act, consult with an attorney in your area. You should also pick up a copy of the *The Living Together Kit* (Nolo Press, Berkeley, California). Here's

> ### ☞ *Hot Tip* • • •
> **B**uying a home out of wedlock? Be sure to include both names on the deed as "joint tenants with right of survivorship," so that if one dies, the other automatically obtains the house. That's assuming you expect to always be together. Otherwise, write "tenants in common" on the deed. More about this in Chapter 7.

what that book has to say. If you're living together out of wedlock, at least do the following:

- Have a will.
- Protect your assets by keeping separate accounts.

Other ways you may be impacted by your unmarried status are:

- If you're not married, you might not be able to adopt.
- In many states, you may not be entitled to unemployment benefits if you relocate because your partner has been transferred.
- If you can provide more than half of your partner's financial support, you may be able to claim him or her as a dependent on your taxes.

Live-in partners also have some credit protections under Equal Credit Opportunity laws and Fair Housing laws. You can't be discriminated against when you apply for a loan to buy a home.

Avoiding Money-Related Stress

We've already told you some of the emotional issues that money triggers in couples. There also may be circumstances beyond your control that can affect your financial situation and add to the stress in your relationship.

But would you believe the mere task of getting yourselves organized in your new marriage can be an additional source of tension? It sure is. You've got to get used to each others' sometimes unusual habits.

Gail: Honey, is there any reason there are half-empty coffee cups sitting around all over the house?

Al: How come there's petrified food in the refrigerator and all the drawers are stuffed with paper dating back to the Revolutionary War?

On the positive side, you can get rid of a lot of paperwork by consolidating some of your savings, credit cards, and investment accounts.

Apart from the obvious, though, it's important to put as much financial planning into your marriage as we hope you did into your wedding.

Newlyweds today tend to be older than they used to be. Men typically marry at age 27, while women marry at 25, reports the U.S. Census Bureau. Because both spouses often are working, they may already own cars and homes, and have established financial identities. Unfortunately, too many of those identities are based upon running up debt. As a result, fear of running out of money has become a paramount national issue for many families—and one that can spearhead too many family arguments.

We Can Work It Out

Best to avoid these issues from the start. Each of you needs to evaluate your own financial mindset and determine what about it you want to discard or retain.

Get things straightened out immediately. Have a family meeting and discuss certain issues. Take these steps:

- Agree from the beginning that financial decisions be joint decisions.
- Set some short-term and long-term financial goals. You'll need cash to cover at least three months' income. Then there's a child's college education, weddings, and retirement to name a few.
- Is one of you seriously in debt? You might want to be sure to keep property separate—to shelter money from the other spouse's creditors. Also, if either of you apply for additional credit, get it based on the financially solvent spouse's income and credit history.

A Couple That Screams Together Can Dream Together

Are your financial objectives the same? Determine what each of you wants to do with your money longer term. In fact, psychologists say you should make "dreaming together" over a ten-year period a regular part of your relationship not just when it comes to money—but in most other areas of your life as well. Say, one of you hopes to save, but the other wants a new pool. Work out an immediate compromise. Neil Clark Warren, Pasadena, California, is a psychologist and author of the book *The Triumphant Marriage*, published by Focus on the Family. He suggests listing all obstacles you expect to encounter in reaching your goals, and then devising a way to deal with each of the challenges listed.

Then, he says, write down how you both will feel once this goal is accomplished. "Designing a dream for your future together is an exercise that every couple needs to engage in—and preferably every year," Warren says.

Here are some other areas to focus on:

- If your hands, like those of most newlyweds (and old married couples) today, are trained to reach straight for the credit cards rather than a passbook, make an early commitment to change. Try to invest any cash you receive as gifts. You'll be glad later on that you did.
- Figure out how much each of you owes on each card, and determine how you will eliminate those balances. Consolidate accounts. Too many cards could prevent you from getting a mortgage.
- It's equally important that you maintain your individual credit ratings by keeping at least one credit card active in each spouse's name.
- Make arrangements for any child support and repayment of loans.
- Jointly agree right away on where you will store deposit slips, canceled checks, and any important receipts or documentation needed for tax records. Take it from us, you'll eliminate many arguments if you both always know where these things are.
- Make an inventory of all your belongings early in your marriage— before you lose any of your receipts or records of wedding gifts. This not only will give you an idea of how much property insurance you'll need, but it will be easier to file a claim if necessary.
- Find the right financial help. Look for a professional with at least ten years of experience that comes highly recommended from friends, your lawyer, or accountant.

- Evaluate your insurance—homeowner's, medical, and life insurance—to determine if it is adequate, or whether it is even necessary. Eliminate duplication, and make certain beneficiaries are changed to reflect your new marriage.
- Insure engagement and wedding rings if they're worth a lot.
- Consider getting life and disability insurance.
- Once you've knocked down your debts, set aside regular savings. Pay yourself first each week and make major house and car purchase decisions only after being sure you can save 5 percent to 10 percent of your household income.
- Try to have at least three to six months' income in a bank account or money market fund. You may need the money if you lose your job or for other financial emergencies.
- Invest for the long term. You can have money electronically deducted from your checking account and put into a bank savings account or mutual fund.
- Review and update your will or trust documents. You need to talk to an attorney about revising your will. A family and children have to be protected. If you expect your net worth to be more than $625,000 (or $1.3 million if your family owns a business) in 1998, consider an estate tax plan. Otherwise, your family risks paying as much as 55 percent in estate taxes when you die.
- Be certain you establish which of you will take care of routine household money-related tasks such as paying bills. Perhaps, as we do in our marriage, for example, one of you can oversee the stock, bond, and mutual fund investments, while the other pays bills and handles real estate.

Identify Sore Spots Early On

If you can spot the sources of money-related tensions early on, you can prevent a lot of family headaches. The hard part is making a change in your personality that may or may not be related to your pocketbook. You may need to rethink your beliefs and actions so you can work together to solve problems.

Here are a few common troublesome areas worth nipping in the bud early on:

- The husband is the breadwinner and handles the family money. The wife may feel helpless, useless, or trapped—a role she doesn't exactly like. Or, the man might treat her as unimportant. Guess what happens? She gets angry. Plus, the man may resent her lack of contribution, and feel unfair pressure to perform. We need some equality here. Running the home is just as important as going to work. Agree in advance on how you will split up the household duties and respect each other's roles.
- The wife earns less than the husband. This not only can hurt a woman's self-esteem, but also result in her exclusion from family money decisions, for which her input is critical. We need a happy balance here. Both partners need to recognize the importance of her input.
- The husband earns less than the wife. That's tough on the man, who "learned" early on that the man needs to be the breadwinner. It also can be hard on the woman, forced to justify her "inferior" choice in a mate to herself and possibly to family and friends. Husbands: Put your ego aside. Pitch in and jointly decide the family financial game plan. Wives: Cast aside these cultural stereotypes and remember why you married this guy!
- You both spend too much. This is a prime cause of stress. Put away or cut up those credit cards. Set up a spending plan. Only spend so much on the things you enjoy. Don't go over the limit. Analyze where you might cut costs on routine expenses. More about this in Chapter 9.
- One of you has to work two jobs to make ends meet. This very tough situation means you both must put your thinking caps on to develop a better life. Analyze your skills to determine what higher-paying careers you might qualify for so you can cast aside one of those time-consuming jobs.

Don't worry if your earnings are unequal. It's just a matter of both spouses placing value on the lower-earning spouse's other talents or contributions to the marriage. Finding that hard to do? Perhaps the higher-earning spouse might consider forking over some extra cash to the other.

Psychologist Michael warns that if women feel financially dependent in a relationship, they tend to be less vocal. "She becomes less willing to stand up for her own opinions." It's not quality of education or financial status either, Michael stresses. In fact, in marriage counseling, it's often a woman's fear of not being able to support herself that keeps her from leaving a relationship. The key, she says, is for both partners to avoid taking their roles for granted. When a marriage falls apart, it very often is because the woman doesn't feel worthwhile in the relationship.

For a man, by contrast, when a marriage disintegrates very often it's because he feels the woman stopped supporting him emotionally.

When men aren't successful, Michael warns, they tend to withdraw and stop communicating. "They use alcohol and activity to make them feel better. They become some kind of a holic, a workaholic, foodaholic, sexaholic, or baseballaholic. . . .

"That's one of the pivotal issues with regard to a break-up during hard times. Women walk out on men when they're not doing well. Also, men act differently if they're not doing well."

While men tend to withdraw, women are the opposite. They like to talk about their troubles—often, when a man doesn't want to be bothered and just wants to relax after a hard day's work. These differences, Michael notes, are major areas that women and men need to work on together. Men need to find ways to communicate what they are thinking and feeling without necessarily talking about their troubles. On the other hand, women need to button up when their men need to relax.

Sometimes, there are events you have no control over. Take unemployment. Scott South, of the State University of New York at Albany, claims that based on his econometric model, approximately 10,000 more divorces occur for every 1 percent rise in the unemployment rate.

To avoid being part of that increase, or anything else related to divorce statistics, it's important, financially, to prepare for these unexpected downturns. As a rule of thumb, it's a good idea to have an emergency fund to last you six months. This way you needn't make unreasonable financial demands on your partner to take care of you. Don't completely rely on your spouse for emotional support in down times either. You may need to look to friends, family, church or synagogue, and resources in the community.

HOW TO COMMUNICATE

Don't argue. Try these tips instead:

- Are you a man who doesn't feel like responding to a woman? Consider a phrase like, "I'm not talking a lot, but it has nothing to do with you." This helps clear the air and make the woman feel better.
- Are you a woman who needs a sounding board for her troubles? Make certain you're not infringing upon your man's need to unwind, try asking, "Is this a good time to talk?"
- Consider offering a little gift in return for getting what you want. For example, a woman might offer a partner, say a backrub, in exchange for being able to talk things out. Or, a man might consider providing a night on the town in return for an evening of peace and quiet.
- Do something active together, like go for a walk or go running. Men tend to work things out in action.

It's important to remember that when you as a couple work on something and resolve it together—whether it be a disagreement, tough times, or a short-term or long-term plan—something unique happens. There's a deep sense of self-pride—couple pride, Michael says. The ending is a happy one, complete with the mutual understanding that neither of you could have reached without the other.

Bringing Home the Bacon

Apart from stress over differences of opinions on money, there are additional money issues that come along with today's society, depending upon who in this blissful union works for a living. Or, perhaps in your particular case, who doesn't. An uncooperative economy also can create some bumpy roads in your relationship. It's only by understanding your emotions about money in each of these different situations that you can take steps to cope.

To Work or Not to Work

Whether one or both of you work largely is up to how you both feel. If you have a child, perhaps one of you would prefer to stay home for awhile. On the other hand, working may be essential for you both to meet your expenses. Working may well add fulfillment to your relationship. While we can't exactly help you with the personal choice of whether to work, we can help if money is involved.

The following table can help you decide whether it truly is financially worth it for you both to work. Sometimes, based on the added expenses of gas, childcare, clothes, and a car, it really isn't.

Figure 5.1 • • • • •

Should You Both Work?

This checklist will at least help you to establish whether that second job in the family truly is worth it:

Weekly take-home (pay after taxes, Social Security, insurance, and pension) _____

Additional expenses if you go to work:
Gas _____
Tolls, cabs, trains _____
Extra car payment _____
Extra car insurance _____
Lunches _____
Daycare _____
Additional cleaning and laundry expenses _____
Additional hair care _____
Additional clothes _____
Maid service _____
Job-related educational expenses and dues _____
Additional miscellaneous expense _____
Total job-related expense _____
Take home-pay less expenses _____

Note: Does the cost of going back to work take a big bite out of the paycheck? If so, it might not be worth taking a job.

Two-Paycheck Couples

Have you made the decision that you're both bringing home the bacon in this relationship? You're not alone. Today there often are more workers in the family than your ancestors ever would have bargained for. With a downsized workforce, many of you are working more hours than you'd like. Plus, you may be fearing for your job. Add a couple of kids and/or elderly parents to this equation and you have the makings of enough stress to sprout porcupine needles on a kitten!

We know how it is. Both of us work. Often, after a hard day's work we're exhausted and feel stressed out. We've gotten into a few spats once in a while ourselves.

When you both work hard for a living and have a lot of financial responsibilities, it's easy to get mad at one another. We have a standing agreement that after things blow over, the one who lost his or her temper picks up the tab for dinner at the other's favorite spot, which as you might imagine, differs dramatically.

Particularly when you have tons of bills to pay, it's easy for tempers to flare. It always seems like the car breaks down at the worst possible time—right after you just paid off your credit card debt. Now you've got to borrow again. Then there are kids to take care of, and they always get sick. To keep yourselves from going stark raving mad, you've got to go out for a night on the town once in a while.

Then again, one of your jobs could force the family to relocate. Or perhaps one of you needs to go back to school at night.

Be prepared—both money-wise and attitude-wise. Estimate the cost way in advance. Then sock away extra cash to help foot the bills.

The family needs to meet to discuss any moves or disruptions your jobs might cause. Children should be encouraged to express how they might feel about going to a new school if you must move. What if one spouse doesn't want to go? Perhaps you can agree to try it for a while and then return if things don't work out.

It's critical, if you're both working, to set aside a time to be together with the family and have fun. Otherwise, you'll all go nuts. It's equally important to schedule meetings to handle the family's money. After all, you probably have more of it than you would if just one of you worked!

Bad Feelings

Boy oh boy. What happens if the wife resents that her husband doesn't have a fatter paycheck? Or if hubby hates it that his wife makes more than he does. There could be "trouble in River City" if you don't share what's on your minds.

Keep resentments to yourselves and they grow into anger and hostility. Before you know it, your happy home on Pleasant Street turns into an ash pile below Mount Vesuvius.

Family therapists suggest nipping problems in the bud by giving each other written lists of what's bothering you. As long as you agree to solving the problems, you can work through the issues with good, hearty discussions. If you can't agree, nothing gets accomplished. You wind up stuck in a rut.

Owen Ryan, a Worcester, Massachusetts-based M.S.W. family therapist, suggests that becoming more aware of how you are acting will help you gain better control of your emotions and make important financial decisions. He suggests the following exercises:

- Keep a diary and write down how you feel every time resentment builds. Write down what happened and how you reacted.
- Acknowledge your feelings before they get out of hand. Notice when you're starting to blame your spouse for money or other problems you may have around the house, and stop yourself. Once again, stating how you feel: "I feel angry or I feel resentful because. . ." should help you recognize the true cause of your anger and make it easier to contain it. Too often we react to our own feelings by lashing out at innocent bystanders in our very own homes.

> ☞ **Hot Tip • • •**
>
> **D**oes your spouse or lover suddenly want to avoid sex? Believe it or not, clinical psychologists say your partner could well be upset because he or she isn't making enough money. If you can't seem to solve your problems, see a good psychologist or clinical social worker who specializes in couples therapy. Colleges or universities in your area often have lower-cost help. If your company has an employee assistance program (EAP), financial or mental health counseling may be included.
>
> • • • • •

The idea is to find what actually is triggering your angry outbursts or your depression. Sometimes money issues can be pretty deep-rooted, and their results can ricochet into other areas of your life.

Good Feelings

On the positive side, though, there are lot of reasons for both of you to hold down jobs.

There's nothing like coming home from a hard day at work feeling you did a good job and accomplished something. You'll make more friends, have more money to save, have more topics of conversation, and enjoy your life. In addition, your children are apt to feel more independent and be forced to take on more responsibility.

In Business Together

More than a half-million couples go one step further than both working. They own their own businesses. This presents a double challenge. Some experts recommend that you don't even attempt a husband-wife business partnership unless you're each on an equal footing. Otherwise, one spouse can wind up giving the orders to the other—a bad scene that can carry from the office to the home.

Meanwhile, if the business fails, as many small businesses do, you lose both your livelihoods.

No matter how strong your love is for each other, spending 24 hours a day with your spouse can be difficult. You have to make sure each of you has some quiet time alone. In addition, you have to divide up the duties of running the business and the household. Better hold a lot more meetings if you're both in charge of getting things done in two places!

But there are a lot of advantages to owning and running your own business. You are the captains of your ship. You are in control of your own destinies. You call the shots and make the profits. In addition, we hear—not only from family business consultants, but also from our psychologist friends—

☞ *Hot Tip* • • •

If you're partners in a business, be certain that you've decided who will run the show when you're no longer around.

If you leave the business to a child, make sure the child wants that role, and has the skills to handle it.

• • • • •

that couples who run successful businesses together may well be the happiest married couples of all.

One-Paycheck Couples

While there's certainly a financial benefit to having a second income, sometimes you have no choice but to earn just one paycheck—especially if a woman wants to take time off to have a baby. We know people who have bitten the bullet because one spouse just had to get away from a lousy job in a bad working environment. Others go back to school to improve their chances of getting a better-paying job. Yet others have inherited a bundle and have the good fortune to go into early retirement.

As we already discussed, our society still has us thinking that the man in a marriage should be the breadwinner. You'll hear antagonistic comments about women who are supporting their husbands while they finish law school or medical school.

Meanwhile, a woman who never has worked has no job skills and may feel useless in her own eyes or the eyes of her spouse, children, or friends. Resentment easily can build if you're not careful, and it soon can be throwing wrenches into your life together.

Whatever work situation you may choose, you need to be able to forget what other people might think and believe that the choice you made is for your mutual benefit.

Even if one spouse doesn't work, that spouse still needs to know that he or she is contributing equally to the household. Perhaps a say when it comes to the family money can help.

EZ Ways to Prevent Financially Stress-Related Marital Problems

Apart from just everyday arguments, there always is something that's going to put strain on a marriage, whether it is having a child, seeing him or her off to college, or your own retirements.

Then there are problems with the in-laws, jobs, sickness, death, and disability, as well as economic downturns, investment failures, and simple investment goofs.

It's no wonder almost half of all marriages fail!

With all life's other stressful periods, it's important to agree at least on one thing: you will work together to manage the family finances to reach your goals. That means going over all those financial statements together, and deciding together what to do with your money.

The bottom line: because you love and trust each other, you both must set financial goals, and keep a positive outlook about money. You don't need to be rich to be financially successful. You merely need to feel that you're doing better this year than last.

H O W   T O   C O M M U N I C A T E

No matter whether one or two of you work. These steps will add financial harmony to your relationship:

good

1. Set aside about one hour regularly and a special place to discuss money. No, not in bed. Some say it should be somewhere around a table where you can sprawl out financial records. Meetings should be in a place comfortable for both of you.

2. Don't be afraid to disagree. Disagreement is healthy—provided you don't start calling each other miserable names.

3. Keep in mind the love you have for each other is more important than any temporary financial setbacks. Life continues—despite all the bills.

Alimony and Children from Previous Marriages—Who Pays the Bills? The Emotions of Financial Baggage

"The second wife always gets the biggest diamond," comedienne Joan Rivers often jokes. But then again, the second wife also has to deal with hubby sending money to his first wife and kids.

There's a whole new set of hurdles for spouses who have remarried—ex-husbands and wives, existing children,

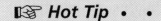 **Hot Tip** • • •

Do not permit a child to get involved with money requests made by an ex-spouse. Deal with former spouses and lovers directly.

• • • • •

Hot Tip • • •

One natural source of stress in a second marriage occurs when an ex-spouse remarries. *Cosmopolitan* magazine serves up some great ways to cope:

- Mourn. Mourning will enable you to say goodbye to a failed marriage.
- Explode. Hit a pillow, yell and scream, or play a ferocious game of, say, volleyball to vent your frustration.
- Write a letter, but don't mail it. Express your emotions.
- Rationalize. While your pain is real it's not necessarily because you've made a mistake. You'll probably feel jealous of the new spouse even if you're currently happy in your new marriage.
- Celebrate the wedding. Do what makes you feel good. Buy yourself flowers. Have a massage. But don't prolong your sadness by thinking constantly about happy experiences in your first marriage.

• • • • •

and former relatives. Unfortunately or fortunately, these people never go away. Women who divorced and had children often were left poorer. It's no wonder that the divorce rate in second marriages is 10 percent higher than for first marriages!

Talk about a source of tension. Most people who marry the second time around are older and have more money. They are used to going out on the town, taking trips, or enjoying the hard-earned fruits of their labor. But nothing can spoil a nice evening at the theater quicker than the memory of your ex (or your spouse's ex!). If you let it get to you, it can take energy away from a new relationship.

Remarry and you had better learn control of your emotions. No matter what your second spouse says before you wed, there's a good chance he or she is going to despise it when you have to send your first spouse alimony.

Then there may be stepchildren. Don't expect stepparents to be too thrilled about supporting a new mate's child from his or her first marriage while the check is going to the first spouse.

Second marriages can be tough. Although you may have some of the above emotions you hadn't bargained for, realize that these are natural feelings in second marriages. In fact, as of this writing, experts were predicting that by the year 2000, families from remarriage will outnumber first-marriage families.

Funny, You Don't Look Like Your Name

You've tied the knot, and you suddenly have an option on your name. When should you take the name of your spouse? When should you keep your own? What are the repercussions of each? Then again, some couples use both spouses, last names, hyphenated. Could that be the way to go? This chapter gives you the legal and financial repercussions of whatever name you choose.

Who Are You? What Is Your "Legal" Name?

Many, men in particular, treat this as a big joke. But if you're a woman, this is an important milestone in determining your true identity, perhaps for the rest of your life. Think about this one. If you choose the wrong name, or you don't clearly choose a name, it can haunt you forever.

Waffle on this issue, and you could find yourself in the situation of one of this book's coauthors. You might have your driver's license in one name, and tax return and Social Security form filed in another.

"Sign your name here," somebody tells you. You have to stop dead in your tracks. What is your legal name? What does it mean? Should you add your spouse's name to yours with a hyphen? Should you take your spouse's name and subtract your own name. What if you've already been married previously? Should you have the last name of two husbands, or go back to your original birth name?

The NOW Legal Defense and Education Fund in New York notes that at least three state attorney generals—in Maine, Michigan, and Wisconsin—have issued opinions permitting men to adopt a woman's name at marriage. Plus, it says, the Equal Credit Opportunity Act gives a woman the right to keep a credit account in her birth surname, her husband's surname, or a combined surname.

Meanwhile, whatever name you take could well influence that of your children. Nobody, it seems, really cares which name you give them—unless the two of you disagree—which, we hope by now, you do less frequently. In disagreements, courts almost always rule in favor of the father, NOW reports.

Deciding on a married name is a tougher call than one thinks. Take the authors of this book.

"Hello, Mr. Liberman?" telemarketers said to the male coauthor, when he married the other coauthor and moved into her Florida condo. "Yes," he'd respond, not wishing to spend the time discussing the error.

Then, he'd get off the phone and grouse to his spouse-coauthor. "Why don't you just change your name?"

So, his spouse did change her name—at least on Social Security and for the IRS and on her medical plan—stuff that nobody sees. The driver's license stayed "Liberman" as did the professional name. It wasn't worth tossing career recognition built up over 25 years, she reasoned.

Problems:

- Doctor's offices would call at work asking for "Mrs. Lavine," only to be told no such person works there.
- Frequent flyer cards in the name of "Lavine," failed to coincide with business-related airline tickets in the name of "Liberman," and frequent flyer miles went uncredited.
- When persons asked for identification, the driver's license—which had a photo—failed to coincide with airline tickets. Fortunately, a hyphenated last name on checks once saved this situation.
- Plus, the whole issue was a point of argument with the male coauthor of this book.

That's not all that can happen. If you're considering using more than one option, consider the friend of ours who reserved tickets to a Broadway show in a hyphenated name—her maiden name and her husband's name—and then forgot. When the couple went to pick up their tickets they mysteriously were nowhere to be found.

Experience incidents like these on a consistent basis and you'll wind up in Bellevue!

A woman's married name affects not only her and her spouse. We've heard of cases in which a spouse's relatives actually were rude because they thought that the woman, who declined to take her husband's name, was not as committed as she should be.

Then, there is the issue of media identification. The New York Times, notes author Peggy Noonan, might have employed one of the strangest style of all—requiring a "Mrs." title on a married woman—even though she has chosen to retain her maiden name.

Name changes can wreak havoc on computer systems. The Social Security Administration in 1996 claimed to have $234 billion worth of wage reports—some dating as far back as 1937—that it was unable to match with individual accounts.

Apart from not knowing what to do with surnames, a report issued by the Social Security Administration's San Bernardino, California district, cited women as being responsible for a large portion of the errors. Women often failed to notify the Social Security Administration when they changed their last names.

Now, the Social Security Administration reports, it has 200 million unresolved wage items in "suspense," representing $250 billion in wages. It suggests that all workers make certain they're getting proper credit for their earnings by requesting a Personal Earnings and Benefit Estimate Statement periodically (see phone number and Web site in Chapter 4).

When a Woman Should Keep Her Own Name

Anyone who thinks social traditions are getting more equitable would get a jolt by a *Bride's* magazine reader survey. The poll revealed that more first-time brides in their 20s are planning to take their husbands' names—87 percent in 1996, compared with 71 percent in 1992.

An American Demographics poll in 1994 indicated that First Lady Hillary Rodham Clinton actually had broken tradition. She was among "just 10 percent of married women in the United States who use something other than their husband's last name. Hyphenated names are used by 5 percent of couples, while just 2 percent of married women use their maiden name. About 3 percent, including Hillary Rodham Clinton, who uses her maiden name as a middle name, opt for other alternatives."

The wives who break with tradition are affluent achievers, the poll said. "That's because achievers are professionals who have worked hard to establish their names in their fields. Other women who keep their own names are in the "fulfilled" group—individualists who view the custom of taking a husband's name as outdated.

Women who marry younger are more likely to use nontraditional last names—14 percent of those under 40 compared with 5 percent for women 50 or older. Women with higher education and incomes are more likely to take a nontraditional name.

Meanwhile, NOW reports that children currently are adopting parents' hyphenated surnames. Also, some parents have named boys with their father's surnames and girls with their mothers'.

Instances in which women might want to retain their own names:

- They are well-known.
- They have a career.
- They marry late in life and are too well-known by their own name.
- Their spouse has a long or difficult name.
- They like their own name better.
- They are frustrated with the male-dominated establishment.
- They want old friends to be able to find them in the phone book without having to know who they married.

When a Woman Should Change Her Name

A woman might consider changing her name:

- When she marries at a young age and has not yet built her career.
- When her husband is well-known.
- When she wants to.

On the other hand, a woman needs to make sure she's also not giving up power along with her name. As we indicated on the issue of money, both parties in a marriage need independence and an equal amount of power. Otherwise problems can result.

How a Woman's Name Affects Her Spouse

Having a spouse with a different last name is a real headache-and-a-half, the male coauthor of this book can testify. Anytime you have to call for information about your spouse, you play a guessing game about which name was used. Typically, the person on the other end of the phone is checking records on the computer. It takes an extra five minutes to get things straightened out or get the information you need.

There is only one real solution to the problem. Pick out one name and use it for everything. Either use your own name, a hyphenated name, or take your husband's name. It really doesn't matter. Otherwise, it's a totally aggravating mess.

Gail: So Al, why did you pressure me to change my name in the first place?

Al: You've been bugging me about this ever since we wrote this chapter. Before we got married I had a lot of friends whose wives either kept their maiden name or used a hyphenated name. They were about as happy as you will ever see people that have been married for more than ten years. So in my mind, it really didn't matter. But then when we got married I got confused. I wanted you to be part of me. I wanted to get as close to you as I could get. I wanted us to merge. I just felt closer to you when I

☞ *Hot Tip* • • •

Steps to take regardless of the name you choose.

- When you get married, decide on your names legally, professionally, and socially. Personal tip from us: If you plan to use a hyphenated name, make certain all important documents use the hyphenated last name, so there is no confusion—no matter how much people laugh.
- If you keep your birth name, obtain a certified copy of your marriage license. Always carry it with you when you leave the country and for important transactions. The coauthors of this book almost were unable to close on a new home because a driver's license contained a different name from the sales contract. A marriage license saved the day!
- If you change your name, notify Social Security (800-772-1213). If you don't have the same name on your Social Security records as on your tax return, you could have problems—including a hold on a tax refund.
- If you change your name, change it on your passport.
- Notify your employer, registrar of voters, state department of motor vehicles, credit card issuers, banks, insurance companies, tax preparers, and frequent-flyer programs of any name change.
- Try to carry at least two photo IDs at all times—one under your birth name and the other under your married name.
- If you use two names, make certain your bank accounts are in both. Have both names printed on your checks.

• • • • •

said Gail Lavine—you were now part of me. Nevertheless, it really doesn't matter if you go by Gail Smith-Jones. I love you just as much.

Changing a Name

There is nothing magic about changing your name. The general rule, the American Bar Association reports, is that as long as a woman uses a certain name consistently and honestly, that's her name.

Notify all government agencies and private agencies that have records of your name of the change. You'll particularly want to be certain you notify the Internal Revenue Service, Social Security Administration, U.S. Post Office, state tax departments, professional licensing agencies and societies, lenders, landlords, banks, credit card companies, phone companies, utility companies, newspapers, doctors and dentists, and schools and colleges you attend or that your children attend.

The NOW Legal Defense and Education Fund claims that most states have formal legal procedures for changing a name. The advantage is it provides a court order and a public record and thus proves to everyone that the name change is legally binding.

PART

Sprouting a Money Tree

Now it's time to separate the money from the love. The trick is to get your money to grow in value without letting spats about money hinder your decisions. Tips in this section will help you avoid the number one money problem that the two of you have control over—not having enough. By joint and careful planning early on in your relationship, you'll not only reach some agreements before you have a chance to argue, but you'll also increase the nest egg you have—no matter how small it might be. Read on...

Chapter 7

For Better or Worse: Sharing Your Dough

Say you fit into this typical mode: One spouse is a spender, and the other is a saver. These characteristics can be the source of many a disagreement. Dividing up the family money, though, goes beyond just who spends and who saves. It also involves who owes what, and what property and money come in and out of your relationship. You can own things yourself or jointly. This chapter examines the pros and cons to both.

Reevaluating Your Accounts and Assets

There's no way around it, folks. One of you thinks the money needs to be handled one way. The other thinks another way. No matter how much you love one another, take it from us: you're likely to have different opinions about the family money. Regardless of how much you have, this can ruin your marital bliss—if you're not careful. We've run into the same headaches from time to time.

Gail: Great! A tax refund. Let's go out to dinner.

Al: Aww. I wanted to put it in our retirement account.

! How to Communicate
. . . . .

● To get things on the right track:

1. Have a family pow-wow to discuss dividing up money.

2. Figure out how much should go into each account.

3. Regularly review your income and expenses and make any necessary changes.

. . . . .

Psychologists we know say it really doesn't matter how you split up your accounts, but how you feel about the way it's done.

Which Accounts and Assets Should Be Joint? Which Separate?

Financial planners say one solution to avoid arguments over who spends what is to split up the money three ways—her checking account, his checking account, and a joint checking account.

The joint account is used to pay for common expenses such as a mortgage or rent, utilities, and food. He feels great because he can use his checking account—or should we say not use it. She also enjoys free use of hers on various and sundry shopping excursions. In other words, each spouse's checking account covers those specific personal expenses that are apt to tick the other off. This way, each is solely responsible for those expenditures. It can foster independent management of money, and each partner can maintain a certain amount of privacy. It can serve to avert many a potential dispute over each other's spending.

With a joint account, you easily can track your monthly living expenses. So, when you need to analyze how to cut costs, you can just grab that checkbook register.

The downside: You probably will have to pay three sets of bank fees. It's also three times as much work. Plus, it can tip the scales on the financial workload in your relationship. So if one of you slips up, there could be fireworks if you start blaming each other.

How much should you put in each checking account? A lot depends on how much you make and whether you are a one-paycheck or two-paycheck couple. Two-paycheck couples should take an equal cut for their own accounts, if possible, and put the rest to cover the family expenses in the joint account.

If one spouse works, or, if earnings are unequal, then it gets tricky. The nonworking spouse may be taking care of the house and the kids—which is just as important as bringing home the money. That spouse may need to be paid equally in his or her own account, or resentment can build.

Your checking account philosophy can work with savings accounts and other investments as well—particularly if you each have different styles of investing.

Having a Single Joint Checking Account

We have three checking accounts. It's easier on both of us. Then one doesn't get mad when the other spends on a personal pleasure.

But we know people who keep just one joint checking account. They feel it's easier to keep track of the money. One person is in charge of the checkbook. He or she pays the bills and gives the other a weekly allowance.

With one account, you only have one set of fees to pay. Plus opening a joint account to commingle all your money can be pretty romantic. It can make you feel cozy. If you have a joint account, either spouse can sign on the account. That's quite an advantage in an emergency. But if you're having problems, or one of you is careless or more prone to debt, there's nothing to prevent one spouse from quietly cleaning the account out. The other can be left with zilch. Meanwhile, you both need to keep a close eye on the balance and be diligent about noting each transaction in the accompanying register. Failure means you've just created one more issue to fight about!

Having a joint account can start out great, but if one of you earns more than the other, the other might have a lingering fear about what happens to the money if you split up. Plus, psychologists warn a joint checking account won't help matters if one or both of you is losing independence—a phenomenon that often starts with the birth of a child. After all, it's your separate identities that drew you together in the first place!

Emotions aside, recordkeeping for a joint checking account can present a unique challenge to any couple—even if you each also have your own account.

Take the message we got from our Family Finance column on America Online from a woman asking what to do about her "sweet but clueless" husband, who keeps overdrawing their joint account.

Here are a couple ways to deal with this problem.

1. Have the husband double up on his responsibility. If it's a case of simply not knowing how to manage money, he can learn and be accountable for his mistakes.

2. This could be a symptom of a deeper relationship problem that needs to be worked on. Could the wife be triggering the behavior? If it's really serious, perhaps the couple should have separate accounts until they can solve the problem, or, they might consider psychotherapy.

> **☞ *Hot Tip* • • •**
>
> **T**o avoid financial and marital headaches with a joint account, make certain you take the following steps:
> - Never write a check without logging it in the checkbook. This goes without saying on any checking account, but it's particularly hard to keep track of expenditures when two people are involved.
> - Don't get an ATM card for your joint account. Take it from us, you'll never get all those withdrawals written down!
>
> • • • • •

Wellesley, Massachusetts financial planner Jane King cautions against joint accounts in general. She advises that where possible, assets should be split equally in each person's name. After all, she says, what happens if both of you happen to die at the same time—certainly a possibility if you travel a lot together. With a joint account and no will, your estate could be left without heirs.

Separate Checking Accounts

If you each maintain your own checking account, spenders get to buy whatever they want (or can afford) without their spouses necessarily knowing. However, this arrangement could feel unfair to one spouse who earns less than the other, yet has a host of other responsibilities around the house. Also, with two separate accounts, it might seem easier to get out of your relationship—a factor that could worry one or both spouses.

On the other hand, if splitsville is in the cards, having separate checking accounts does not legally protect you quite as much as you might think. State laws differ, and many often guarantee a certain amount to a spouse in the event of divorce—regardless of whose name it's in.

Expect to have to do a lot of math in your relationship if you have separate checking accounts. You'll probably have the hassle of splitting everything down the middle whenever you make a purchase. Meanwhile, if you can't share your money with each other, you might also have trouble sharing your feelings and your love.

Oh, Those Credit Cards!

A credit card can be a great instrument—provided that you pay your balance every month. Getting into the habit of not paying it off monthly is what leads to the financial ruin of many otherwise-happy couples.

Late payments and missed payments go on your credit record. So if your spouse has had a credit problem before you got married, you might want to think twice about having joint credit cards.

One way to avoid the perils of credit card debt is to get a joint American Express charge card. You must pay the full balance due. It's a disciplined way to make purchases. Then you can pay the bills out of your joint checking account.

Don't want your wife to know you spent $300 on a Big Bertha Titanium driver so you can hit your tee shots 250 yards straight down the middle of the fairway? Or don't want your husband to know what it cost for that Ferragamo pair of shoes? Better to have your own credit cards. But be sure to pay the bills off quickly—preferably every month.

How many credit cards should married couples own? Keep the number low, please. One joint card, plus a Visa or MasterCard in each of your own names, should be plenty.

Meanwhile, it is critical for women, in particular, to retain some sort of credit card during a marriage. Otherwise, if anything happens to her spouse, she may find herself with no credit. A woman opening a joint credit card can ask to have her record reported to credit bureaus in both a maiden and married name.

CDs and Other Deposits

The FDIC and National Credit Union Share Insurance Fund (NCUSIF) typically insure deposit accounts to $100,000 per person. However, joint accounts, IRAs, and trusts are each separately insured to a maximum of $100,000. So if you and your spouse have a joint account, that translates into $50,000 worth of insurance per spouse.

Say you and your spouse have two joint accounts, one with $100,000 and another with $25,000. Only $100,000 is covered.

However, both the FDIC and NCUSIF combine balances depending on your share of ownership. So if you have a joint deposit account of $80,000, each of you has a $40,000 share eligible for insurance coverage and can insure another $60,000 in joint accounts with other immediate family members.

Cars

You generally can reduce your car insurance premium if you put more than one family vehicle on the same insurance policy. Plus, with both names on the policy, there's no question about coverage and benefits if either of you is involved in an accident.

Safe Deposit Boxes

If you are like most couples, you probably have a safe deposit box together. Contrary to popular belief, in many states, if one of you dies, the other can get the contents out of the box. But make certain you ask your banker what the rules are in your state before you get a safe deposit box or decide what to put in it.

What if you each have a safe deposit box? Each of you probably should have a key to the other's box. Make sure a person you trust has your bank's approval to gain access to the contents in the event of a crisis or if both of you suddenly die.

No need to worry about your company's safe deposit box. Corporate safe deposit boxes are not sealed at death.

Keep in mind that a safe deposit box may not be quite as safe as you think. Even though they are generally lodged in a bank, the contents are not FDIC-insured. So make certain you read the contract you sign when you rent the box to determine if any insurance is provided. Some banks may make a very limited payment if the box or its contents are destroyed or damaged. If you're concerned about the safety or replacement of valuables in the box, you might consider fire and theft insurance. Often, such insurance already is part of your homeowners or tenants insurance policy, so check your existing policies first.

If a bank fails, the acquiring institution typically would take over that bank's offices, including locations with safe deposit boxes. If the FDIC conducts a payoff because no acquirer is found, box holders would be mailed instructions about removing the box's contents. Stolen property may be covered by what's called a "blanket bond," a multipurpose insurance policy a bank purchases to protect itself from fire, flood, earthquakes, robberies, and embezzlement.

Should You Have Joint or Separate Property or Investments?

This area gets particularly tricky. Not only do you have to consider love, emotions, and finances, but also, children, past marriages, and taxes.

Too many couples buying a home listen to their real estate agents on how to own a property, we hear from Emily Card, a Santa Monica, California attorney and coauthor of *Managing Your Inheritance* (Times Business). Bad move. "Real estate agents may not consider issues like estate planning." Better to have an accountant, financial planner, or lawyer help you out on these issues, she tells us.

The big question in determining the type of ownership is whether you want the person you own it with to own the property when you die.

Three General Ways to Own Property

Typically, the type of ownership must be written on the deed or ownership documents in intimidating terms that have been carried down from the Middle Ages.

"Fee simple" or "sole ownership." This means you own the property or investment exclusively. You, the single owner, can do whatever you want with it. You can sell it or give it away. This is a great way to leave an asset that has increased in value to an heir so that he or she can avoid the capital gains tax, currently 20 percent, when sold.

The glitch: with this type of ownership, you probably should have a will and a lawyer to probate the will. Plus, if the total value of the estate is at least $625,000 (increasing annually to $1 million in 2007) your heirs still may be stuck paying estate taxes, which can range from 37 percent to as much as 55 percent of the estate's value.

"Joint tenancy with right of survivorship." This is the most common way husbands and wives own property, although it needn't be limited to husbands and wives, nor restricted to two people. Each of you can give your interest away or sell it—provided that you both (or all) agree and share in any profits. When you die, the property automatically goes directly to the surviving partner or partners, so you avoid

> **☞ Hot Tip • • •**
>
> **N**o need to worry if your spouse or partner dies in debt if property is held as joint tenancy with rights of survivorship. Creditors can claim the debtor's share of a joint tenancy only if they move to claim it before the debtor's death.
>
> • • • • •

probate. When property is left to a spouse, no estate taxes are due immediately. Upon death of the second spouse, though, both the income and estate tax collectors can take their cuts.

Experts say that although most married couples opt for "joint tenancy with right of survivorship" when it comes to their assets, they risk paying capital gains taxes on inherited property that way.

This stuff gets pretty complicated. Nevertheless, here's how it works: When the first spouse dies, the surviving spouse inherits half of each asset at the owner's market value, but still owns half at the original price paid. Say the original price of the asset bought 20 years ago was $10,000, but it's worth $20,000 at the time of a spouse's death. If the property is sold, the current 20 percent capital gains tax is due on half—$5,000—of the $10,000 profit. That's $1,000 in taxes.

"Consider holding assets in sole ownership with the husband and wife each owning roughly half of what the couple has," suggests Diana Kahn, a Coral Gables, Florida-based certified financial planner. "Then when the first spouse dies, the surviving spouse receives 100 percent of the inheritance at the current market value. If the survivor sells assets after the death of the first spouse, he or she will be able to keep more of the profits."

"Tenancy in common." With this form of ownership, which also involves two or more people, you can own part of the property and still give your heirs a capital gains tax break. Each "tenant in common" operates just like a "sole" or "fee simple" owner, and probably needs a will. When you inherit property this way, you could pay estate taxes if the value of your estate is greater than $625,000.

Community Property States

As we've mentioned earlier, most property acquired by either spouse during a marriage is considered owned by both spouses in nine "community property" states and in Puerto Rico. Community property states are Arizona, California, Idaho, Louisiana, Nevada, New Mexico, Texas, Washington, and Wisconsin.

Meanwhile, an estimated 24 of the remaining states offer their own answer to "community property" laws through an optional form of ownership known as "tenants by the entirety." Limited to married couples exclusively, "tenancy by the entirety" offers greater protection because it generally prohibits either spouse from selling the asset without the other's permission.

Insurance: Looking Out for Number Two...

When you were single, you were pretty limited in your insurance needs. Some health insurance, disability coverage, and homeowners' or renters' insurance probably did the trick. But now that you have a spouse and possibly a family to consider, insurance takes on a whole new significance. Unfortunately, insurance probably is one of the most aggravating financial instruments you'll ever have to attempt to decipher. This chapter seeks to make insurance, which serves as the underlying foundation for your financial life together, easier to understand.

What Kinds of Insurance Do You Need?

Malcolm Forbes, the late editor and publisher of *Forbes* magazine, took good care of his family. When he passed away, his loved ones collected on a whopping $70 million insurance policy, which replaced the money the estate had to pay out in taxes. It's no wonder his son, Steve Forbes, was able to run for president in 1996. He had plenty of money.

Unlike the Forbes family, most of us aren't billionaires. Over our lifetime, we might make $1 million, if we're unusually lucky. So we really need to protect our families.

It's critical first that you have adequate health insurance coverage, either at work or individually. Next in line is disability insurance. Disability insurance protects your income in case you are injured and can't work. If you are starting a family, you also will need life insurance. Plus, you may need extra disability coverage if you don't get enough through your job.

Those getting up in years might consider long-term care or nursing care insurance, which we'll discuss in greater detail in Chapter 14.

If you don't know anything about how insurance works, it can be very confusing. Besides that, you have to sit around the dining room table with your spouse, and maybe your kids, and talk about being injured or dying—not exactly your favorite subjects.

! H O W   T O   C O M M U N I C A T E

Insurance can be a major turn-off—particularly when salespeople come in and talk to you about death and illness. But psychologists say it's important to prepare yourself for these issues. So it's appropriate to pull the family together before you're getting ready to meet with an insurance salesperson.

1. Be open and express your feelings on the subject.

2. Talking about the death of a loved one? It's OK to cry. In fact, expressing your feelings brings the family closer together, while burying them can lead to feelings of depression and unhappiness.

3. Remember the positive. You're taking steps for your family's future well being.

Health Insurance: Stuff It Covers

No doubt you already know the importance of medical insurance. If your union has brought two different policies into the family, now may be the time to weed one out. One of you might find you do better on the other's policy.

Before you discard any insurance policy, or take on a new one for that matter, you need to know the basics. Many health insurance companies pay the hospitals and doctors directly. You receive a copy of the bills.

As you probably already know, you typically have a deductible on your policy. In other words, you have to pay your own expenses up to a certain level, say $250 or $1,000, before your insurance company will pick up any of the tab. After the deductible, the insurance company may pick up a percentage, say 80 percent of the tab, and leave you paying the rest—at least until you reach a certain threshold. Major objectives: to get the lowest threshold of out-of-pocket expenses possible, keep your deductible low, yet pay as little as possible each month.

Does your policy have basic hospitalization? This covers doctors fees when you are in the hospital, surgery done both in and out of the hospital, room and board, and nursing services. Also covered are X-rays, lab tests, blood transfusions, and drugs and medications. Typically, you're also covered for tests done outside the hospital.

Major medical coverage picks up some of the tab that basic hospitalization does not cover. It pays for doctors, specialists, osteopaths, and chiropractors. Also covered: the cost of outpatient treatment and drugs plus medical supplies such as wheelchair rentals, respirators, and prosthetic devices. Ambulance, x-rays, and lab expenses prescribed by the doctor often are covered.

What about a TV and telephone in your semiprivate room? Unfortunately, you'll have to pay those out of your own pocket.

Types of Plans

Today it's been estimated that more than 25 percent of the population receives managed care coverage through Health Maintenance Organizations (HMOs). Plans offered through groups or an alliance typically are less expensive than individual policies. HMOs are made up of a group of doctors who are paid a salary rather than a fee-for-service. You or your employer pay a monthly fee, known as a "premium," to use the medical services of the HMO.

Once you pay your premiums, you can use HMO's medical services either free of charge or by making a small "copayment" for each doctor visit. Copayments can run from as little as $5 to $25, depending on the plan. Many HMOs may require you to go to a primary care physician. This doctor, depending on the plan, may be responsible for making referrals to an HMO specialist.

Preferred Provider Organizations (PPOs) work like an HMO, but are more expensive because they allow you to go to a doctor or hospital on the plan without obtaining a referral. You'll pay more, however, if you go outside the PPO's network.

Disability Insurance

If you're supporting a family, better make sure you check out disability insurance—particularly if it's not among your employer's benefits.

Once again, in return for payment of a monthly premium, you should get a benefit of 50 percent to 70 percent of your gross income covered.

The cost of coverage can be expensive. A nonsmoker, age 35, with a gross income of $50,000 would pay about $1,200 a year to get $25,000 in income coverage.

You can lower the cost of the coverage by selecting a 90-day waiting period before you receive the disability income.

☞ *Hot Tip* • • •

- Because hospital stays are typically less than one week, look for an insurance policy that pays hospital bills from the first day you're hospitalized.
- Try to avoid policies that exclude mental illness, elective medical procedures, nongeneric drugs, etc.
- Make certain you are with a financially strong health insurance provider. Weiss Research (800-289-9222) provides company ratings for a nominal charge.

• • • • •

☞ *Hot Tip* • • •

When shopping for disability insurance coverage, it's important to consider several important criteria:

- Compare policy premiums.
- Your policy should be noncancelable and guaranteed renewable. This means the policy can't be changed or canceled without the policyholder's consent.
- Many policies give you the choice of collecting benefits for two, five, or ten years, or all the way up to age 65. Best, if possible, to opt for the long term—up to age 65.
- Try to select a policy with a cost-of-living adjustment. This way, disability benefits should rise as inflation increases, but your premium stays the same.
- Get a policy with "residual value." This means you still can collect if you can work only part-time.
- You also should have the option to increase your coverage as your income rises— despite any medical problems you may have.
- Buy only from the financially strongest insurance companies, which carry ratings of at least A+ by A. M. Best & Co., and AA by Standard & Poor's or Moody's.

• • • • •

Life Insurance

Now that you're a family, life insurance also becomes particularly important. You'll certainly want your family permanently protected if you're no longer around, right? If you have children, don't ignore life insurance just because you have no income. Somebody will have to watch the kids if you're not around.

Almost 98 percent of people who apply for insurance get it, but persons who are already ill or are in high-risk professions might have a harder time qualifying.

What Types of Policies Can You Pick From?

Term insurance. Term insurance provides limited protection for a specified period, although some policies are renewable. If you die while the policy is in effect, your beneficiaries collect the designated face amount. For a few hundred dollars a year, a younger policyholder can insure his or her family for a hefty sum at a relatively low cost. You can buy term insurance that is annually renewable or renewable every 5, 10, or even 20 years. DRAWBACKS: Unlike other forms of insurance, which give you a savings component, term insurance merely gives you insurance coverage (you can't borrow against the policy). Plus, you generally can expect your cost to rise at renewal.

Whole life insurance. This is a more permanent form of life insurance. Your monthly premiums fund a specific death benefit. But the amount left after covering the cost of insurance and expenses goes into a savings account, known as "cash value," that the insurance company pays interest on over the years. This little kitty grows, tax-deferred. Also, you can obtain a low-rate loan on the policy taxfree.

Insurance companies pass on excess earnings on whole life to policyholders in the form of dividends. Typically, dividends are used to purchase more insurance, so you can reduce the number of years you must pay premiums.

There are several types of whole life insurance. "Straight life" is the most popular because you pay level premiums over the years. You get a relatively large amount of permanent protection for your premium dollars because expenses are paid over the life of the contract. DRAWBACK: Whole life typically pays relatively low rates on the cash value.

> ☞ **Hot Tip** • • •
>
> **S**ome term policies actually are convertible into whole life policies. Many plans will allow you to exercise this convertibility feature without another physical exam.
>
> • • • • •

Universal life insurance (UL). As with whole life, your cash value account grows tax-deferred and you can obtain a low-rate loan against it taxfree. This policy actually combines term insurance with a savings account that generally is higher-yielding than that offered by whole life insurance. Your cash value earns market rates paid by the insurance company that typically track the bond market. Or, if you'd prefer to invest in stock and bond mutual funds directly, you can buy a variable universal policy. With variable universal life, you, rather than the life insurance company, decide when to buy and sell money market funds, bond funds, and various types of common stock mutual funds. DRAW-BACK: Your cash value changes with the performance of your investments, but you're always guaranteed your death benefit.

With universal life, you can vary your premium payments and death benefit to coincide with your financial condition.

Policy Riders

Insurance contracts can be set up through "riders" to cover you for special situations. It may cost you an extra $50 to several hundred dollars per year per rider. So be careful. The extra cost depends on the insurance company, your age and health, and the size of your policy. Here are some of the frequently used riders.

- Guaranteed insurability rider. This lets you increase your insurance coverage without having to take a medical exam or buy a new policy.
- Disability income rider. This tacks on some disability insurance coverage if you're unable to get it elsewhere.

Bet You Didn't Know

• • • • •

Whether you buy a whole life, universal, or universal variable life policy, you benefit from the following attractive features:

- Your investment grows tax-deferred. You can withdraw the premiums you paid for the policy over the years taxfree. Withdraw more than the total of the premiums paid, however, and you pay taxes on the earnings.
- You can borrow against 80 to 90 percent of the cash value in the policy taxfree. An attractive feature of all cash value polices that allow cash value build-up is that you can obtain a low-cost loan.
- You get a minimum guaranteed rate on your cash value, which ranges from about 4 to 4$\frac{1}{2}$ percent at this writing.

• • • • •

- Double indemnity or accidental death benefit. This means if you die in an accident, the survivors collect double the death benefit. Some policies also cover dismemberment.
- Automatic premium loan provision. This rider is designed to cover your premium payments in a financial emergency. The insurance company pays the premiums as a loan against the policy's cash value.
- Waiver of premium. This waives your monthly life insurance premiums if you get injured or disabled. It is not designed, however, to be a substitute for disability insurance, which covers your income.
- Family riders. This lets you buy family term insurance with your whole life coverage.

How Much Coverage Do You Need?

Most people need about five to eight times their current income for life insurance protection. To get a quick and dirty estimate, multiply your yearly wages by five or eight. Example: Are you making $50,000 a year? You may need between $250,000 and $400,000 of coverage, depending on the size of your family.

Hot Tip • • •

Life insurance is expensive. The more you can save and invest over the long term, the less insurance you may need.

• • • • •

It's best to sit down with an experienced insurance professional to develop a well-thought-out insurance plan that looks at how much you need to take care of your spouse, children, and in some cases, your parents.

Seeking Professional Help

There are three important ingredients in finding the insurance policy that's right for you:

1. Deal with a well-trained insurance professional.
2. Stick with a financially sound insurance company.
3. Compare the cost of insurance policies before you sign on the dotted line.

Here are the different kinds of professional designations that financial professionals might have:

- Certified Financial Planner (CFP). The CFP designation is awarded by the Certified Financial Planner Board of Standards (CFP Board) Denver, Colorado, to candidates who have completed intensive financial planning coursework, passed a national examination, have three years of experience and abide by the code of ethics.
- Chartered Life Underwriter (CLU). Any insurance agent worth his or her salt has a CLU or is working toward getting this designation. And if you find a person with both the CLU and Chartered Financial Consultant (ChFC), you know this person has a strong background in insurance and all aspects of financial planning. Both designations are issued by the American College, Bryn Mawr, Pennsylvania, to individuals who have passed a national examination based on at least a dozen courses related to financial planning.
- CPA, Personal Financial Specialist (CPA, PFS). This designation is given to CPAs who pass a stringent financial planning examination administered by the American Institute of Certified Public Accountants.

Find a Strong Insurer

Whether you buy a term insurance policy, whole life policy, or universal variable policy, it's important to evaluate the financial strength of the insurance company. You want to be sure that the company will be paying your loved ones the money they need when you are not around.

The financially strongest companies carry A+ and A++ ratings by A.M. Best. Also review the insurance companies claims-paying ratings by Standard & Poor's, Moody's, and Duff and Phelps. Companies rated at least AA in claims-paying ratings are considered best. With Weiss Research, a stricter source for ratings, insurers above B are considered financially sound.

Comparing Policies: Coverage and Fees

Unfortunately, it's tough to figure out your insurance costs because of all the different charges involved.

First, be sure that when you compare policies of different companies, you're comparing apples to apples. Each quote should factor the same age, premium payments, and policy type.

Keep in mind that when you deal with an insurance agent, your first-year commission can be as high as 55 percent of your premium. Over the next two or three years, it often runs about 5 percent. After that, it averages about 2 percent. You can save on these commissions by purchasing insurance directly from these no-load companies: USAA Life Insurance (800-531-8000), Ameritas Life Insurance Corp. (800-552-3553), and John Hancock Marketplace (800-555-1440).

There also are a host of other fees and expenses. The bottom line is to compare two things: (1) The premiums you pay, and (2) the "cost comparison index." This index tells you the average yearly net cost per $1,000 of insurance protection. The lower the number, the lower the cost of your insurance coverage.

> ☞ **Hot Tip** • • •
>
> You can get an insurance company's financial rating from your insurance agent, the public library, or by contacting the rating agencies directly by phone at:
>
> - Standard & Poor's (212-208-1527). There is no charge.
> - Moody's (212-553-0377). There is no charge.
> - Duff & Phelps (312-368-3157). There is no charge.
> - A.M. Best (908-439-2200). There is a $2.95 charge.
> - Weiss Research (800-289-9222). There is a $15 charge to get the rating over the phone. A written rating costs $25.
>
> • • • • •

How Your Beneficiaries Get Paid

You have a number of choices how your beneficiaries can receive the money from your insurance policy when you die. Your insurance agent can help you decide on the best alternative.

Interest option. The insurance company keeps the money and pays the beneficiary interest on that amount. The beneficiary gets payments every one, three, six, or twelve months.

The beneficiary may have flexibility to take out part or all of the proceeds in cash—if that's the contract you set up.

Installment payments. Your beneficiaries get a monthly check from the insurance company. The insurance company guarantees the proceeds.

> ☞ *Hot Tip* • • •
>
> The Consumer Federation of America (202-387-6124) has a life insurance evaluation service that's helpful. CFA's charge is $40 to rate the first policy and $35 for each additional policy. You can write the Consumer Federation of America (CFA) at 1424, 16th St. NW, Suite 604, Washington, DC 20036
>
> • • • • •

This can be set up in a few different ways. For example, with a life income option, the beneficiary receives the income for as long as he or she lives.

If the surviving spouse is willing to settle for less monthly income, he or she can leave the balance of the insurance money to his or her beneficiaries for a set period of 10 to 25 years. Your insurance agent calls this "the life income period certain option."

Money Isn't Everything— Sometimes It Isn't Enough

More than one million people are filing for personal bankruptcy annually. Could you be next on the list? We hope not—particularly because you're in love. Debt problems become even doubly difficult to handle when two people are involved, and they ricochet into relationship problems when emotions take hold. If just one of you has some financial trouble, a minimum of two of you suffer. Do you already owe more than you make? Acknowledge it now. This chapter will help you zero in on any financial problems and give you tips on banishing them from your lives together—forever, we hope.

Are You in Hot Water?

Fortunately people don't go to debtor's prison nowadays. It's a good thing. If they did, we'd see some pretty notable people behind bars. Think your financial headaches are triggered simply by not having enough money? Wrong. Just look at actor Burt Reynolds. He recently was reported to have $6.6 million in assets. You'd be pretty content with that, right? Not Burt. His debts were published at $11.2 million.

Rapper M. C. Hammer was estimated to have earned $33 million in 1990. Yet, guess who filed Chapter 11 bankruptcy? Yup. He did.

And 1976 Olympic gold medal winner Dorothy Hamill divorced her husband of eight years, Kenneth Forsythe, whom she blamed for poor management of her affairs. She declared bankruptcy in 1996. Now, we don't need any of these problems in our lives, do we?

If you think you might be in financial trouble, we suggest taking this test designed by the National Foundation for Consumer Credit.

☞ *Hot Tip* • • •

While some pretty wealthy people are in financial trouble, it doesn't take much income to get rich. Tom Stanley and Bill Danko, authors of *The Millionaire Next Door* (Longstreet), found that a person who smoked three packs of cigarettes a day for 46 years would have become a millionaire if he or she had invested that money in Philip Morris stock during that period instead.

• • • • •

1. Is more than 20 percent of your take-home pay used to pay credit card bills and other debts, excluding your mortgage?
2. Is your savings account shrinking?
3. Do you charge things impulsively?
4. Are you approaching the limits on your credit cards?
5. Are you paying the minimums on your charge cards?
6. Have you defaulted on a rent payment more than once?
7. Are you getting calls because you're late paying the bills?
8. Do you plan to use your raise to pay off debts?
9. Are you uncertain about how much you owe?
10. Are you considering consolidating your loans to pay off those credit cards?
11. Are you using the cash advance on one credit card to pay off another card?
12. Are you charging more each month than you are paying off?
13. Are you paying bills with post-dated checks?
14. Are you one who does not consider credit as a form of debt?

If you answered yes to just a few of these questions, take it as a warning sign that you may be in financial trouble and could be a prime candidate for bankruptcy.

**Bet You
Didn't Know**

• • • • •

If you're having serious debt problems, consider these sources for help:

- The National Foundation for Consumer Credit is nonprofit organization with more than 850 affiliate offices nationwide. The affiliate offices are known as Consumer Credit Counseling Services (CCCS). Call 800-338-2227 for information on the CCCS in your area. While the organization often offers free or low-cost counseling services, it is funded, in part, by creditors. It also may charge a fee for administration of your debt restructuring program.
- Family Service America is an international nonprofit group that can refer you to nonprofit centers in your area that provide credit counseling as well as other family-related services. Call 414-359-1040 or visit http://www.fsanet.org to find a center near you.
- Debtors Anonymous is a self-help group set up like Alcoholics Anonymous. People with financial problems meet weekly in a self-help group that aims to help people cope with and solve their debt problems. For more information, write General Service Board of Debtors Anonymous, P.O. Box 20322, New York, NY 10025.
- Financial planners in your area. Financial planners are trained professionals who carry the designations Certified Financial Planners (CFP) and/or Chartered Financial Consultant (ChFC). These planners will help you control your spending, encourage you to refrain from borrowing money, and help you deal with your creditors. A financial planner worth his or her salt will help you set up a payment plan with your creditors. Keep in mind, however, that many financial planners make their money from selling life insurance or investments. Coming out of debt, financial planners can help you set up savings and investment strategies.

• • • • •

Cooperating on a Budget: How to Compromise

Whether you're in financial hot water or not, the first step to getting your relationship on a solid financial footing is for you both to recognize one important principle: You need to stop borrowing money and start saving to get anywhere fast financially these days. Perhaps it's time to make this matter the focus of a special meeting between the two of you.

Are either of you carrying a balance on one or more credit cards? Consider making a pact to stop using them. Credit cards are magnificent critters—but only as interest-free loans for those who pay their full balance each month. Otherwise they can totally destroy you financially, and hurt your relationship at the same time. Next time you go to charge a blouse or jacket, stop and think. What about going for a walk or a work-out in the gym instead? Or consider paying cash. You'll automatically be more aware of your spending.

The next step is to get yourself out of what we call the "I don't know where it's all going" syndrome. This simply involves analyzing where your money is going, and where spending can be cut and/or redirected. You might think you know where you're spending your money. But it's not until you put it down on paper that you can see ways to change your habits.

This isn't as difficult as it sounds. Look at your checkbook register over the past year and itemize your sources of income and expenses. (If you're using a computer-based program this will be even easier. It will not only give you totals, but will draw graphs to show you where your money is coming from and where it is going.)

Now for the hard part. After you have looked at your cash flow, you have to zero in on your wasted spending and set up a plan to save. Just a minute, please. No need to slash your throats right off the bat.

Start by looking at your spending habits line by line. You've probably already resolved to cut your debts. But there are other things you can do to free up cash to pay off more bills. Once you've gotten yourselves out of debt, you can focus on building up your nest egg, saving for your child's college education, which we'll go into further in Chapter 13, and your retirement, which we'll help you out with in the next chapter.

But first, compare your spending habits with suggested limits in the table opposite. This way, you'll get a feeling as to exactly where you're going a little overboard.

Figure 9.1

• • • • • •

Budget Worksheet

Income versus Expenses

	Monthly	Yearly
Income:		
Wages	_____	_____
Investment income	_____	_____
Other (rent, alimony, child support, etc.)	_____	_____
Total Income	_____	_____
Expenses:		
Housing:		
Rent or mortgage	_____	_____
Utilities: electric, oil, gas	_____	_____
Water, garbage, sewer	_____	_____
Telephone (list local and long distance separately)	_____	_____
Personal:		
Food	_____	_____
Clothing	_____	_____
Personal care	_____	_____
Other	_____	_____
Auto (list separately for each vehicle):		
Car payments	_____	_____
Repairs	_____	_____
Gas	_____	_____
Tolls	_____	_____
Licenses	_____	_____
Parking	_____	_____
Other	_____	_____
Medical:		
Doctor	_____	_____
Dental	_____	_____
Optical	_____	_____
Drugs	_____	_____

Figure 9.1

• • • • •

Budget Worksheet (cont.)

Insurance:	Monthly	Yearly
Auto	_____	_____
Health	_____	_____
Homeowner's	_____	_____
Life	_____	_____
Disability	_____	_____
Other	_____	_____
Entertainment:		
Vacation and travel	_____	_____
Dining out	_____	_____
Video rentals	_____	_____
Other	_____	_____
Other Expenses:		
Banking and brokerage fees	_____	_____
Childcare	_____	_____
Child support	_____	_____
Credit card and loan payments	_____	_____
Donations	_____	_____
Education	_____	_____
Gifts	_____	_____
Hobbies	_____	_____
Dues	_____	_____
Newspapers, books, subscriptions	_____	_____
Pets	_____	_____
Allowances	_____	_____
Other	_____	_____
Savings:		
Bank or credit union	_____	_____
Mutual funds	_____	_____
Brokerage	_____	_____
IRA or pension	_____	_____
Total Expenses:	_____	_____
Total Income less Total Expenses:	_____	_____

Source: *Improving Your Credit and Reducing Your Debt* (New York: John Wiley & Sons, 1994, pp. 151-53. Adapted from Gail Liberman and Alan Lavine.)

Figure 9.2 • • • • •

How Spending Habits Stack Up

How do your actual spending habits stack up against your spending plan? This worksheet provides suggested proportions of your aftertax income each category might represent.

Monthly Progress on Budget

(% of after tax income)	Proposed Spending Plan Limits	Actual Spending
Housing (25%)	_____	_____
Food (14%)	_____	_____
Life insurance (6%)	_____	_____
Transportation (7%)	_____	_____
Installment debt (less than 20%)	_____	_____
Entertainment and travel (6%)	_____	_____
Clothing (6%)	_____	_____
Savings (5% or more)	_____	_____
Medical (varies)	_____	_____
Utilities (varies)	_____	_____

Cutting the Waste

Before you bring down the hatchet and cut all the enjoyment out of your life, figure out all the painless ways you can cut everyday expenses without necessarily cutting back on the things you like to do. Here are a few examples:

- Buy brand name goods at discount factory outlets. Wait for sales at your favorite store.
- Do more haggling. People have always negotiated the price of their autos. Try it with that new washing machine, refrigerator, or air conditioner.
- Clip and use coupons when you go grocery shopping.
- Take advantage of specials.
- Avoid long distance phone calls.
- Increase insurance deductibles.
- Take your lunch to work (it'll probably be healthier, too).
- Food shop on a full stomach to ward off impulse buying. Replace expensive meats, cold cuts, and steaks with pastas, chicken, rice, and veggies.
- Cut down on expensive paper products or buy them in bulk.
- Shop at resale shops.
- Are you dining out too much? Try cooking at home more.
- Read magazines at the public library for free.
- Barter. Give your neighbor a terrific meal in exchange for a car tuneup or a haircut. What can you do well? What can your friends or neighbors (or relatives) do well?
- Look into consolidating auto insurance with your spouse.
- Take a vacation off-season near home instead of flying off to the Bahamas.
- Consider buying in bulk by joining a warehouse such as Costco or Sam's Club.

You Need a Cash Management Game Plan

Apart from just cutting back on obvious items, advisers say you can save a bundle simply by managing your cash a little better. That includes pricing bank services, maximizing interest income by depositing and writing checks at the proper time, and by making better use of credit services.

Find a bank, thrift, or credit union that has the best combination of fees and rates on checking and interest-bearing accounts. Check monthly fees, particularly if required balances aren't maintained. You can be zapped with fees ranging from $3 to $30 per month. If you have your accounts linked, sometimes you can be charged on every account if combined balances drop below a threshold. These charges can add up pretty dramatically after a year. Why not shop around? There's probably no need to be paying these fees nowadays, given the number of institutions that offer free checking accounts.

Other financial institution fees to compare: overdraft charges, stop payment charges, safe deposit box costs, wire transfer fees, and money order or cashier's check fees.

Bet You Didn't Know

• • • • •

Here are some ways to save money by simply managing your cash a little better:

1. Pay off installment debts before you invest. The cash in the bank is earning low rates while you may be paying up to 21 percent on your credit cards.
2. Avoid using "foreign" ATMs. It can cost 50 cents to $2 every time you use an ATM not owned by your bank. Tapping a regional or national network five times a month would cost you $45 and $60 a year, respectively.
3. If possible, make tax-deductible contributions into your IRA or company 401(k) pension plan. Expect a tax refund? File early and use it to fund your IRA. You have until April 15 to get tax credit for the prior year.
4. Pay up-front mortgage fees via a separate check to your lender so that they are tax-deductible.
5. Don't overpay the IRS on tax withholding. It's money you can invest at a profit. If both you and your spouse are employed, the IRS recommends that the spouse with the higher salary take all the withholding allowances. That way, your withholding will be closer to your actual tax liability.
6. Don't buy U.S. Treasury bonds, notes, or bills from your broker. It will cost you between $25 and $50 per security in fees. You can save by investing directly with the Federal Reserve Bank in your region. For free information on buying Treasury Securities, write the Bureau of Public Debt, Department F, Washington, DC 20239.
7. Consider tax-free municipal bonds if you are at least in the 28 percent tax bracket.
8. Sock away all you can in your company pension plan. If you're at least in the 28 percent tax bracket you can save from $280 to $391 in taxes for every extra $1,000 you invest in your company or nonprofit organization's pension plan.

• • • • •

Save money by shopping for no-annual-fee credit cards with grace periods, and paying off your bill every month. But make sure that you're not charged a fee for paying on time. Also, watch out for whopping late fees if you don't pay your credit card bill by the due date.

Corporate treasurers deposit checks right away and pay bills at the last possible moment to earn the "float" or interest on money until a check clears. Why not try these tactics on yourself? It might sound like pennies here and there, but these dollars add up by the end of the year and can go a long way toward painlessly reducing your bills.

If you maintain a $1,000 balance in your interest-earning checking account, a direct payroll deposit can mean an extra $6.15 a year. Couple that with paying your bills at the end of the month instead of at the beginning, and you may be saving an extra $16 a year. In addition, you can take advantage of the weekend to stretch the float. Saturday and Sunday are not considered business days. Make certain the recipient receives payment on Wednesday. Reason: the check will not clear until the following Monday—that's a full five-day float on which your money is still earning interest.

You also can use the concept of float with money market mutual funds. Money funds usually require that checks are for a minimum amount, normally $250 to $500. So you could write a money fund check and deposit it into your interest-earning checking account. Then pay a big bill with a bank check. As a result, you will earn an extra three to five days interest until the checks clear.

You also can save more money by managing your money fund, bank CD, and money market accounts more effectively. Invest only in no-load mutual funds and save 2 percent to 8 percent in commissions or $20 to $80 for every $1,000 you invest.

The Pros and Cons of Debt Consolidation

Should you consolidate all your debts—roll everything you owe into one big loan? There are plusses and minuses to loan consolidation.

You can save a lot by consolidating your charge card debts into one loan. A rule of thumb: it could be a good idea when the consolidated payment is less

! How to Communicate

· · · · ·

Call regular meetings on money-saving strategies as a part of your ongoing relationship. Consider this agenda:

1. Take a close look at what both of you are spending, write down your income and expenses as we outlined earlier.

2. Brainstorm ways to cut your costs and bills. Make certain you both agree to compromise.

3. Write down common expenses you might cut to get the ball rolling on a positive note. For example, perhaps one of you can volunteer to call your phone company and utility companies to see what lower-cost plans they might offer. You'd be surprised at how easy it is to switch!

4. Depending upon how bad your debt is, you might each have to give up something. Remember you are working on a common goal. Example: maybe one of you can spend less money on those magazines at the supermarket checkout counter in return for one less trip to a ball game by the other. Work your way down your written budget and take turns presenting ideas.

5. Write down the steps you've agreed to take to curb spending. Set them aside for a few days. Tally up how much more money this will put into your pocket.

6. Once you see how much you are saving and how easy it is, you might find it easier to make additional cuts, and then focus your efforts on developing an investment plan.

· · · · ·

than the total of all your payments. It really helps when you lower the average interest rate you pay on your debts.

For example, say you want to pay off $5,000 in debts over three years: See Figure 9.3 for your monthly payments and total interest charges on the consolidated debt, and how you can lower them.

There are several ways to consolidate your loans.

Low-rate credit cards. Many banks are aggressively promoting lower-rate credit cards. So if you qualify for the loan, you can roll the high-rate credit card debt into a lower-rate card.

Be aware that credit card loan interest isn't tax-deductible. Many credit cards charge variable rates. So if interest rates rise, your low-rate credit card could turn into a high one. Remember to figure in annual fees, if any.

Collateralized bank loan. Another way to consolidate debt is to obtain a collateralized bank loan. You borrow the money from the bank to pay off your

---

Figure 9.3

• • • • •

Interest on Consolidated Debt

Rate	Monthly Payment	Total Interest Paid
18 percent	$181	$1,507
14 percent	$171	$1,152
9 percent	$159	$724
8 percent	$157	$640

other debts. You will pay about $1\frac{1}{2}$ to 3 percentage points above the prime rate for the loan. The prime rate currently is $8\frac{1}{2}$ percent. You must, however, secure the loan with other assets like cash, securities, or life insurance. In addition, the loan interest isn't tax-deductible.

Home equity loan. The bank has your house as collateral. You pay about $8\frac{1}{2}$ percent for a home equity loan and you can borrow up to $100,000 or more. Interest on your home equity loan is tax-deductible.

Beware that you can lose your home if you don't pay the loan. Also, a home equity loan often comes with a host of steep up-front fees such as appraisal, filing, and title insurance fees that could make up for some of that interest savings.

Refinancing. Refinancing can be attractive when today's rates are two percentage points less than your current mortgage loan.

Look carefully, though, at the loans you plan to pay off with a home loan. If they are shorter-term loans or loans that can easily be paid off early, think twice about transferring your debt. You're turning these shorter-term debts into longer-term loans, often as long as 30 years. As a result, you might lower your payments, but you will be paying a lot more interest in the long run.

Although consolidating your debts is an excellent way to reduce your monthly payments of both principal and interest, it may not be a good idea if you are teetering on the edge of bankruptcy.

Before you act, talk to your accountant or attorney. When you consolidate, you might be turning unsecured credit card and installment debt into secured debt. As a result, your creditors might take the assets you used as collateral if you go bankrupt.

But if you consolidate your debts by refinancing the house or tapping the home equity line of credit, you may be protected. Under the Homestead Act of your state, part or all of your home may be an exempt asset in the event of bankruptcy. Be sure, though, that you consolidate

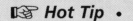

☞ *Hot Tip* • • •

If you must declare bankruptcy, most states let you keep your wedding ring. However, lawyers warn that you better be up front about declaring it as one of your assets!

• • • • •

your debts into the home loan when you are solvent.

You also can borrow from your company pension plan to pay off other debts. Employees can borrow against the vested balance up to a maximum of $50,000 at low rates. In most cases the loan must be paid back within five years. The loan interest isn't tax deductible. Most companies automatically deduct from your weekly paycheck to pay back the loan.

If you have serious financial problems, a debt consolidation loan often can hurt your situation rather than help it. Many lenders charge steep fees or higher rates to persons who have had credit problems. Better off just biting the bullet and get your spending under control.

☞ *Hot Tip* • • •

Some ideas to erase your debt:

- Take on second jobs—at least until your debts are under control.
- Downsize your home. Use any profits you make from the sale of your home to pay off debt.
- Halt use of all credit cards.
- If you have a large home, perhaps you can rent out a room.

• • • • •

Secrets to Agreeing on a Happy Financial Life Together

Insurance in place. Debts under control. Now you can start thinking about enjoying your hard-earned money. Your retirement may be years away. But if you start now, you'll be a lot happier later on. Ditto for some of the other needs you'll have—your children's college education, for example. A new car. Weddings. Vacations. Yes, you can have it all—no matter how little you make. All it takes is a little planning. So get out the paper and sharpen your pencil. This chapter should help you get started on the right track.

Achieving Your Goals with Mutual Funds

Mutual funds are some of the most popular low-minimum investments that can help you reach your goals. A mutual fund is a pool of money run by an investment company with the goal of making its shareholders a profit. Mutual funds can invest in stocks, bonds, or "cash," which actually are debt instruments with maturities no greater than 90 days.

Why should you consider mutual funds—or any other security for that matter? As long as you invest in a well-managed mutual fund over the long-term, say ten years or more, you should make more than you would in the bank. Over the past seven decades, stocks have averaged 10 percent annually, bonds close to 6 percent annually, and money funds close to 4 percent. That's more than CDs, which have averaged around $3\frac{1}{2}$ percent.

Unfortunately, though, there is no Utopia when it comes to earning quick bucks. If you decide to try some of these investments, you need to be aware that over the short term, you can lose your shirt!

But you can minimize your losses by dividing up your money carefully. Historically, stocks have proven riskier than bonds, and bonds riskier than money funds. So, if you need your money soon, it pays to invest in lower-risk securities—or keep that money in the bank!

By developing a long-term investment plan taking these factors into consideration, you slowly can accumulate wealth.

To get you going, here are a couple of benchmarks to give you an idea of how much you must save. They assume your savings earns 8 percent and pays you 8 percent annually.

Bet You Didn't Know

• • • • •

Just when interest rates rise and you might think you're doing great on your investment, you actually can lose money if you've invested in bonds and you're not careful. That's because of a phenomenon known as "interest rate risk." When interest rates rise, bond prices fall.

You also can lose if the entire stock or bond market tanks. Whatever you invest in is apt to move in the same direction as the market.

Bad news about a company or industry can send your investment into a tailspin. Or, a company you've invested in could go out of business and default on its debt, a risk that Wall Street big boys call "credit risk."

Of course, whenever you invest, the complete opposites of any of the above nightmares also may happen, and you could make a killing!

• • • • •

- Say you're looking to earn $22,500 annually in 20 years. You'll need to accumulate $225,000 and save $4,917 a year to reach that goal in a tax-deferred investment.
- Looking for an annual income of $37,500 in 20 years? You'll need to amass $374,000 and save $8,173 a year.

- Want to earn $52,500 annually on your investments? You'll have to amass $523,000 over the next 20 years and save $11,429 a year.

Types of Investments

The longer you have to invest, the more you should invest in stocks or stock mutual funds. But when you approach and hit retirement, you'll want safer short-term investments. We'll slot out your "investment life" below.

- If you're just starting out in the work world, go for the gusto. You'll be investing for 25 to 30 years. So it could pay to put 100 percent in stocks or stock funds. But split it up as much as you can among a small company stock fund, growth and income funds or growth fund and an international fund.
- When you are in your peak earnings years and have about 15 years to retirement, you have to play it safer. A stock market plunge could put a serious dent in your nest egg, and it may take a longer time to recover. So keep about a 60 percent stock fund/40 percent bond fund mix. On the stock side, invest in a growth fund, growth and income fund, and/or international fund. On the bond side, split your investments among an intermediate-term bond fund and a money fund.
- When you hit those retirement years, keep about 30 percent in a well-managed growth and income fund or growth fund and an international growth and income fund. Invest 55 percent in an income fund that pays high dividend yields, and a bond fund. The rest should be invested in a money fund in case you need the cash.

He Says We Need This Much. She Says That Much

Now that you have a feel for the concept of investing, it's time to consider the sad saga about retirement. Most of us will have to work past age 65 to be able to retire. Don't expect things to get any cheaper by that time either.

! HOW TO COMMUNICATE

· · · · ·

To make your retirement together more pleasant, resolve to make the following pact:

1. Start discussing how you both feel about retirement. At what age would each of you like to retire? Will one or both of you continue to work? This will help give you an idea of how much time you have and how much money you'll need to put away.

2. Own your own home if possible. By the time you retire, your home should be paid off or nearly paid off, cutting down on a good chunk of your living expenses (more about this in Chapter 12).

3. Determine exactly how much you'll need to retire at the age you've each determined you want to retire. We'll show you exactly how to do that later on in this chapter.

4. Figure out how much you'll each need to put away monthly to meet that goal. Again, read on for help with this calculation.

5. Start early. Your retirement should take priority over funding your children's college education and other objectives.

6. Periodically assess your progress toward your retirement goals.

7. Regularly analyze your spending (see Chapter 9) to see where you can cut your expenses and reroute savings to retirement.

· · · · ·

In fact, just the opposite is likely to happen. If inflation grows 5 percent a year, $60 worth of groceries today should cost $120 in 20 years. Then, of course, there are all those who predict the doom of what could be our one and only safety valve—Social Security. Even Uncle Sam projects that the Social Security system will be paying out more than it is taking in by the turn of the century.

Now, we don't like to be too pessimistic, but it could well pay to start agreeing about ways to save for retirement early on. That might not be easy when your mailbox constantly is being flooded with catalogs from Bloomingdale's, Saks, and Macy's. So let's cut through the clutter and get down to dollars and cents.

What Social Security Brings to the Table

Today, Social Security replaces about one-third of your income. Unfortunately, we'll probably need about 70 percent of our current income when we retire to maintain our standard of living.

What you might run up against is a gap between your Social Security income and income from any pension or retirement plans you have. This is the amount you'll need to save on your own.

As of this writing, the maximum amount a wage earner at age 65 could receive monthly from Social Security was $1,326. A widow or widower receiving funds from a spouse's account would get the same. If, however, you begin to withdraw your money early—at age 62 to age 64 $1/2$—you'd get a lot less. A 62-year-old wage earner would get a maximum of about $1,061 from Social Security, or 80 percent of what he or she would have gotten at age 65. A widow or widower, collecting on a spouse's account would receive 71 percent or $751.

As we said earlier, obtain an advance estimate of your benefits by calling the Social Security Administration (800-937-2000) and requesting form SSA-7004. You also can get a copy at your local Social Security office.

Think you'll need more than the amount Social Security is apt to provide? Figure 10.1 shows what you'll have to sock away each month just to get an

Figure 10.1

• • • • •

What to Invest to Have $100,000 at Retirement

Years to Retirement	Monthly Investment
10	$575
15	307
20	219
30	114

extra $100,000 at retirement—assuming the investment grows at an annual rate of 8 percent.

A worksheet later in the chapter will help you figure out more specifically how much you're likely to need to save to fill the gap. As you can see, the earlier you start, the less you have to put away each month.

Sorting Through the Gobbledygook: IRAs, 401(k)s, and Annuities

While you may not necessarily be able to bank on Social Security, you can put money into an IRA or other type of retirement savings account to help build a worry-free retirement. In fact, more tax incentives—encouraging people to save for their retirement—were signed into law in mid-1997.

Don't get confused about these terms. They are not investments in and of themselves. Each simply refers to a type of tax shelter.

Often, you can choose which types of investments go into these tax shelters, and financial institutions often determine which of their investments they will permit under these programs. Typically, they have steep U.S. government-mandated penalties for withdrawal before age 59½, as well as tough rules on when you must withdraw.

Meanwhile, inside the tax shelter umbrella, your investment itself may have its own withdrawal penalties, loads, or "surrender charges." Because these instruments are designed to be long-term investments, some financial institutions may offer special incentives to get your business. There might be better rates or lower minimums to open them than there would be if you opened the same investment outside one of these plans.

The best thing about retirement savings accounts, like IRAs, is that contributions may be tax-deductible and/or tax-deferred. Tax-deductible contributions actually are subtracted from your income in the year they're taken, so that you get to pay less in taxes that year. With tax-deferred investments, your earnings aren't taxed until you withdraw.

You may get to take advantage of both of these tax breaks if you open an IRA and have no other pension plan, or if you earn less than a certain amount annually. Not a bad deal!

Then, when you retire, you pay income taxes on the money you withdraw, while the remainder of the investment continues to grow tax-deferred.

> ☞ *Hot Tip* • • •
>
> **C**all the IRS for free publications on retirement savings rules at (800-829-3676). Ask for publication number 560, *Retirement Plans for Small Business,* and number 590, *Individual Retirement Arrangements.*
>
> • • • • •

In all of the above retirement programs, even if your investments are not tax-exempt, you always have the advantage of tax deferment. The savings tax deferment can bring are staggering. For example; if you're in the 28 percent tax bracket and you put $2,000 annually in a tax-deferred account for 20 years and earned 8 percent annually, you'd have $98,846.

If you save the money outside an IRA in a taxable investment, you'd have just $54,598. That's a big difference!

IRAs

With an IRA, you actually control your investments, but you'll be socked with a 10 percent penalty if you withdraw before age 59$\frac{1}{2}$—unless the withdrawal meets one of these three conditions:

1. It is used for higher education.
2. It is made for a first-time home purchase.
3. You are unemployed and need the money to pay for health insurance.

That penalty is over and above any withdrawal penalties or termination fees the financial institution might impose on your IRA. You can invest IRA money into your choice of bank CDs or savings accounts, stocks, bonds mutual funds and American Eagle gold coins, or other bullion coins. But before you consider any of these, check with your bank, broker, or investment company to make certain they have the ability to set up your desired investment as an IRA.

Fortunately, Uncle Sam allows any taxpayer who has earned income but doesn't contribute to a company pension plan to make tax-deductible contributions to an IRA. Single taxpayers can put $2,000 annually into an IRA and get a dollar-for-dollar deduction on their income taxes. Married couples that file joint returns can salt away a maximum tax-deductible contribution of $4,000.

However, the deduction is phased out or eliminated entirely, based on income, for taxpayers who already have a pension plan. The phaseout, which in 1998 starts at $30,000 for individuals and $50,000 for married couples, was slated to increase until they reach $50,000 for singles by the year 2005, $80,000 for married couples in 2007.

Another type of IRA, known as the "Roth IRA," starting in 1998 allows you to invest up to $2,000 a year. Unlike the original IRA, the Roth IRA does not allow you to deduct your contribution from income taxes. However, you can withdraw tax-free if you've maintained it for at least five years and you withdraw under one of these conditions:

☞ Hot Tip • • •

If your spouse has a pension plan through a job and you don't, you still can qualify for a tax-deductible IRA.

• • • • •

You've turned 59 1/2; in the event of death or disability; or for a first-time home purchase. Plus, unlike the original IRA, the Roth IRA does not require you to start taking withdrawals at age 70 1/2.

Eligibility for the Roth IRA starts to phase out for individuals earning adjusted gross incomes of $95,000 and couples with adjusted gross incomes of $150,000.

If you take advantage of a one-time provision that allows you to roll over an old-fashioned IRA into a Roth IRA before 1999, you get to spread the income out over a four-year period for income tax purposes. To qualify, you must have an adjusted gross income under $100,000 in the 1998 tax year.

Simplified Employee Pension Plans

Simplified Employee Pension Plans or SEPs are expanded IRAs for the self-employed. As with IRAs, SEP plan holders can invest in bank accounts, stock, bonds, and mutual funds, and can deduct contributions from their taxes. If you own your own business, you can sock away more into an SEP than an IRA. Your employees also have the option of saving through the SEP plan.

This plan is called "simplified" because it's easy to set up. You fill out a form similar to that for an IRA. Like with IRAs, you control the investing. Each year, you can contribute up to 15 percent of your income or $30,000, whichever is less, into this tax-deferred retirement savings plan.

Keogh Plans

A Keogh is a more flexible retirement plan for the self-employed than a SEP. You can contribute more to a Keogh than either a SEP or IRA. Depending on how it is set up, you can contribute 25 percent of your income annually to a maximum of $30,000. Like other retirement plans, Keogh contributions are tax-deductible. A Keogh can be set up as a profit-sharing plan or a plan that pays a specified income after you retire.

To start a Keogh, though, you may have to hire a lawyer to file a written pension plan with the IRS. There also is a lot of recordkeeping to do. Annual IRS forms must be filled out. Plus, the IRS requires a lengthy report every three years.

401(K) 403(b), and 457 Pension Plans

These are all known as salary reduction pension plans because your taxable wages are reduced by your contribution; so you therefore have less income to report to the IRS. The 401(k) plans typically are used by people employed by larger companies. The 403(b)s are used by those who work for nonprofit organizations, and 457s are for state and municipal employees. Depending on the plan, workers usually agree to put up to 10 percent of their wages into their mutual fund pension plan investments. The maximum amount you can contribute is pegged to inflation. In 1997, you were able to contribute no more than $10,000 into your 401(k). Employers also are permitted to make matching contributions. Typically, employers pay from 25 cents to $1 dollar for every $1 a worker invests.

> ☞ *Hot Tip* • • •
>
> **E**mployee retirement programs, including 401(k)s, often require you to decide on an investment each year by a certain deadline. Miss that deadline and you could wind up earning a piddling 5 percent or less in your 401(k)'s money fund.
>
> • • • • •

Annuities

An annuity is a contract with a life insurance company. You can make periodic payments or deposit a lump sum in an account that earns tax-deferred interest until funds are withdrawn. Then you can take the money all at once from an annuity or receive a lifetime income. Annuities also are a way to avoid probate.

When you start receiving a monthly check from your annuity, you are "annuitizing" the contract. The insurance company agrees to pay you the income for as long as you live. Meanwhile, as with other types of insurance policies, you can pass on some of the proceeds when you die in exchange for lower monthly checks. With one of the most common types of contracts, called "10 year certain and life," the checks are sent to your designated beneficiary after you die for the remainder of that ten-year period.

Only your earnings from the annuity are subject to federal taxes. Each annuity payment you receive is taxed proportionately, based on the value of the annuity and premiums paid. If you withdraw from an annuity before you reach age $59^{1}/_{2}$, you must pay the IRS a 10 percent penalty. In addition, you'll pay income tax on earnings.

Annuities come in several shapes and sizes. The most common are discussed below.

Deferred fixed annuities. This annuity pays a fixed rate of interest, adjusted at set intervals (e.g., annually, or every one to ten years). Fixed annuities currently yield from 5 percent to more than 7 percent, depending on the term to maturity.

With a fixed-rate annuity, the insurance company pays you interest based on the performance of its investments. Say, for example, all the assets of the insurance company earned a total of 9 percent for the year: After the company subtracts the cost of doing business and a margin for profit, it may pay you 7 percent. Remember, there's nothing to prevent the rate you earn on a fixed-rate annuity from declining after a couple of years.

Deferred variable annuities. You may invest in a stable of stock and bond mutual funds. Your funds are placed in a separate account from the insurance company's pool of assets, and the investment risk falls on you.

The advantage of this type of annuity is that you control your investment decisions. If you are willing to assume risk, you can attain higher returns over the long term. But you typically pay additional fees for this benefit. Annual charges run about $2\frac{1}{4}$ percent, according to Morningstar Inc., Chicago. In addition, you pay administrative charges, maybe a state premium tax, and mortality fees.

Meanwhile, if your mutual funds perform poorly over the longer term, you may not have the kind of retirement kitty you expected.

Immediate annuities. If you're already retired and need life-long income, you can invest a lump sum and begin receiving payments immediately over the rest of your lifetime. When you die, your beneficiaries will inherit the balance of the money if you elected that payout option when you signed the annuity contract. Immediate annuities may be fixed, paying you a flat rate for the life of the annuity, or variable, paying a return based on the performance investments you select.

Bet You Didn't Know
• • • • •

An annuity can give you an additional 15 years of tax-deferred earnings when compared with a traditional IRA. With an annuity, you generally don't have to begin taking money out until age 85.

By contrast, with an IRA if you don't begin taking money out by the time you reach age $70\frac{1}{2}$ you get hit with stiff fines from the IRS: 50 percent of the difference between what you take out and the amount required by law.

• • • • •

Of course, there is no free lunch when you invest in deferred annuity. Both fixed and variable annuities typically have back-end surrender charges that can run as high as 6 percent in the first year if you withdraw your funds early. That's in addition to each annuity's built-in expenses.

The assets in a variable annuity are not subject to any of the insurance company's creditors' claims, while a fixed annuity investment, a direct obligation of the insurance company, could be.

Regardless of whether you select a fixed or variable annuity, the annuity's guarantees are only as good as the insurance company behind it. To insure that you are doing business with a financially strong company, make certain it has at least an A+ rating by A. M. Best.

How Much to Save for Retirement

Once the Social Security and retirement plan part of your financial house is in top shape, you must figure out how much income you'll need when you retire.

Your pension and Social Security, as mentioned above, should give you about 60 to 70 percent of the income you have before you retire. That may sound like you're taking a pay cut. But nearly 25 percent of our wages goes to job-related expenses. You'd be surprised how much you spend to look sharp and feel sharp! Particularly if you work with your hands or by the sweat of your brow, you probably go through lots of work clothes.

When you retire, you'll be happy to learn you don't have to worry about all that. You won't have commuting expenses and may only want one car. So, if you bring in 60 to 70 percent of your income, you're doing fine.

Figure the Money You Need

To get a fix on how much you need for retirement fill out the worksheet in Figure 10.2. It will help determine how much extra you need to save, assuming that inflation increases at 4 percent a year.

Figure 10.2 • • • • •
How Much You Need to Save for Retirement

1. How much annual income do you need when you retire?
   Figure 80 percent of your current income.   _____

2. How much Social Security will you get a year? Call the Social
   Security Administration at 800-772-1213 and ask for a request
   for Earnings and Benefits Statement. The report will tell you
   how much you will get based on what you've already paid in.   _____

3. How much will you get from your pension plan at work?
   Get that number from your employer.   _____

4. What's the savings gap or short-fall? Line 1 minus line 2 and 3. _____

5. How much will you need to fund your retirement, assuming
   we have inflation? Multiply your answer on line 4 by an
   inflation factor of 14.3 if you are age 65 or over, 16.5 if you
   are age 55 to 64, and 18.3 if you are age 45 to 54.   _____

6. How much have you saved already, excluding your company
   pension? IRA, Keogh, or SEPs 401(k)
       Annuities
       CDs   _____
       Savings accounts   _____
       Mutual funds   _____
       Total savings   _____

7. What is the estimated value of your total savings from line 6?
   Multiply line 6 by the inflation factor B, listed in the table
   below, based on the number of years you have remaining
   to retirement.   _____

8. Amount of retirement money you need. Line 5 minus line 7.   _____

9. How much do you need to invest each year to reach your goal?
   Multiply line 8 by the inflation factor C, listed below, based on
   the number of years you have to retirement.   _____
   Note: If your employer pays matching contributions into your
   401(k) plan, you can subtract the amount of that contribution from your total.

Figure
10.2

• • • • •

How Much You Need to Save (cont.)

Inflation Factors for Lines 7 and 9

Years Until Retirement	Factor B	Factor C
6	1.27	.151
8	1.37	.109
10	1.48	.083
12	1.60	.067
14	1.73	.055
16	1.87	.046
18	2.03	.039
20	2.19	.034
25	2.67	.024
30	3.24	.018
35	3.95	.014
40	4.80	.011

Source: Scudder Investor Services, Inc. from the Scudder Investor Series

Chapter 11

Knocking at Heaven's Door: Estate Planning Stuff

OK, you're not quite Rockefellers yet. But do you own a house, a car, some jewelry, and/or at least one collectible? If you've answered yes to any of the above questions, you're on your way, we're pleased to inform you, to needing some estate planning. Even those marbles or the Monopoly game you used to play when you were kids are starting to add up in value. If you don't write a will or set up a trust, Uncle Sam will be glad to claim his share. However, wouldn't you really prefer that any valuables go to the object(s) of your affections? This chapter is dedicated to making certain that they do.

Where There's a Will, There's a Way

Perhaps the better title for this section is The Grateful Dead and the Ungrateful Living. Believe it or not, almost two-thirds of us die without leaving wills. It's not just the woebegotten average working couple who are negligent. The late billionaire Howard Hughes and reknown artist Pablo Picasso are among those who never took the time to draft a will.

Abraham Lincoln may be regarded as one of the best presidents we ever had. But when it comes to estate planning, he flunked. He might have had a way, but he had no will.

Don't be like Jerry Garcia, lead singer of "The Grateful Dead," either. He had a will, but that's about it. When he died at age 53 with a $5 million estate, dozens of people demanded a piece of that pie. His wife got one-third, and the rest went to children and managers. Unfortunately, as brilliant a performer as he might have been, he failed to protect his estate from the IRS. So his heirs had to cough up some extra change.

Later in this chapter, you'll see how Jackie Onassis, by contrast, took great pains to see that her loved ones were taken care of, while her estate taxes were minimized.

A will is a legal document that determines who will manage your estate, who will get your property and belongings, and who will become guardian of your minor children when you die.

If you die without a will (called intestate), the state will determine who gets what and who will take care of your children when you are not around.

Along with a will it's a good idea to have your lawyer prepare a durable power of attorney and a living will. The durable power of attorney delegates the power to legally handle your business and financial affairs should you become disabled or incapacitated.

> ### ☞ Hot Tip • • •
>
> It's possible your estate plan may consist of one simple will. However, if you own property and investments, you could need more. It's always a good idea to consult an attorney or financial planner about your estate.
>
> • • • • •

If you fail to select a trusted person to exercise this power, no one will be able to access your bank account, securities, or any other property in your name without resorting to lengthy (and expensive) legal proceedings.

You also may want a living will, which allows you legally to express your preference for continuing or discontinuing health care should you later become incapacitated. A separate document, known as a designation of health care surrogate, names a trusted relative or spouse to make health care decisions for you in case you are physically or mentally disabled.

When it comes to estate planning, don't forget to discuss the issues with your loved ones—even though it's a pretty depressing topic.

You'd be surprised to find out that many adult children don't know where their parents put their wills or whether they have made any plans to reduce estate taxes. Children don't bring it up because they feel parents still are in control. Or they may feel unworthy of receiving an inheritance. Parents and

❗ H O W   T O   C O M M U N I C A T E

● When it comes to estate planning, don't just have a spur of the moment family meeting over dinner. It's too easy to duck out of. Make it official through these formalities:

1. Set a time and place to meet.

2. Designate one member of the family to take notes.

3. "Now's a good time to take care of the grandchildren," might be a good opening line for the first meeting.

4. Talk about how much the estate is worth and who's getting what. Discuss all options available, many of which are discussed in this chapter.

5. Assign each family member a specific aspect of the estate to investigate the best options on how to handle it.

6. Set another meeting to discuss findings and solidify final arrangements.

children perceive estate planning as too closely related to death. Or parents may have fears about treating children fairly.

Yet, lacking important information on estate planning can only add taxes, confusion, and financial uncertainty to your family's hurt when you finally kick the bucket.

Going One Step Beyond a Will

Trusts, which attorneys say are a bit more flexible than wills, have been gaining popularity as estate planning tools.

Trusts enable you to save money by foregoing probate and letting you leave money directly to your heirs. Some types of trusts can reduce your estate taxes and provide income to your spouse or children. However, these goals also might be accomplished by a will, and a trust is not always the right move. A trust, like a will, is a written legal document. You have your money and other assets managed by a trustee so that your heirs get your assets when you die.

Trust and estate tax laws are complex. So before you act, seek the advice of an experienced attorney that specializes in trusts and estates.

Types of Trusts

There are three trusts commonly used in estate planning. A description of each, its strengths and drawbacks, are discussed here.

Revocable living trust. You control a revocable living trust and can change the terms of the trust at any time. You can manage the assets. Or you can hire someone to manage the money based on the trust's instructions. In addition, you can distribute the assets in the trust to your loved ones, or you can keep the money in the trust for as long as you

Bet You Didn't Know
• • • • •

For more information on estate planning write the American Association of Retired Persons at 1909 K St., NW, Washington, DC 20049. Also, you might check with your insurance agent or accountant for free information on estate planning. Contact your state's bar association for a list of lawyers who specialize in estate planning.

• • • • •

want. DRAWBACK: Not all of your assets can be put in a living trust. You might have to have a will for other property like cars, household items, and jewelry. You can't get a mortgage from some lenders if the home is included in a family or living trust. Plus, although you avoid probate cost when you have a revocable living trust, the assets in the trust are considered part of your taxable estate. So you could be in for a large tax bill if your estate is sizable.

Irrevocable trust. You can reduce the tax bite, in addition to avoiding probate, with an irrevocable trust. But the terms of an irrevocable trust can't be changed. A trustee manages and distributes the assets of the trust based on the trust document. You give up ownership of any asset you placed in this type of trust. That's why you save on taxes. Legally, the assets are considered gifts to your beneficiaries. DRAWBACK: Once you establish an irrevocable trust, you can't change the terms of the trust. You're stuck.

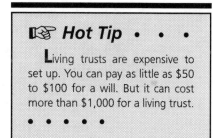

☞ Hot Tip • • •

Living trusts are expensive to set up. You can pay as little as $50 to $100 for a will. But it can cost more than $1,000 for a living trust.

• • • • •

Testamentary trust. Testamentary trusts are used for special situations. For example, say you want to establish a fund to pay for your grandchildren's education, but feel they might squander the money. With a testamentary trust, you can see to it that they're taken care of. The will, containing instructions, goes to probate, and the trust is set up. A trustee then takes control of the assets and disburses them according to your instructions. In this example, money is not given to the grandchildren but their schooling expenses are paid. Assets in a testamentary trust are considered part of your taxable estate because you've had control of the money during your lifetime.

Tax Planning for Naysayers

You could be very wrong if you think you'll never have enough money to worry about estate taxes.

The number of taxpayers subject to estate taxes was expected to grow to almost 45 percent by the close of this century—from 80 tax filings per thousand taxpayers to 115 per thousand in 1999.

Plus, when you factor in your home and personal belongings, chances are you're worth a lot more than you think. Or, at least, you could be worth a bundle sooner than you think.

Starting in 1998, taxes were required to be paid on estates worth more than $625,000. New tax laws were to raise the amount that's exempt over ten years, including 1998, to $1 million. If you own a family business or a farm, you qualify in 1998 for a $1.3 million exemption.

The inheritance tax ranges from 37 percent to 55 percent on estates worth more than $3 million. On top of that, there also may be state inheritance taxes. Could you and your loved ones ultimately get socked with a big estate tax bill? Particularly if you've got a good ten years to retirement, the value of your assets could increase substantially. So sit down with your accountant or financial adviser and look at the numbers now.

Jackie Kennedy Onassis had a "charitable lead trust" set up so that most of the estate was exempt from estate taxes. It was designed so that her grandchildren would receive about 8 percent of its original value in income annually for 24 years after her death, yet shelter 97 percent of the money from the estate taxman.

Even though you may not be worth $600,000-plus yet, we think it's always a good idea to be prepared. Here are a few things to know if and when you have to hire an estate planning adviser:

- As we indicated earlier, based on the new tax laws in 1998 you're probably in the clear for the first $625,000. Federal tax laws permit you to give away a total of $625,000 without paying inheritance tax when you die.
- Fortunately, you can leave everything to your surviving spouse and avoid these dreadful taxes. In tax lingo this is called the "marital deduction." However, when the second spouse dies, Uncle Sam could take his cut.
- You can cut estate taxes with a trust. One way to avert the IRS is to leave $625,000 to your spouse and put the excess money into a bypass trust so that whichever spouse survives receives income for his or her lifetime. No estate taxes are paid, and the money ultimately goes to the heirs of the last spouse, taxfree. This is a complicated and possibly

expensive legal maneuver, so please consult an experienced attorney.

- Consider second-to-die life insurance coverage. While both spouses are still here, some financial planners suggest purchasing second-to-die life insurance and putting it into an irrevocable trust. The insurance proceeds are not subject to estate taxes. When the last spouse dies, the death benefits are used to pay the estate tax bill and the property goes to the heirs. You must make large premium payments for this policy, so be sure to do business only with a financially strong insurance company. Strong companies carry at least an A+ rating by A. M. Best and at least AA claims-paying ratings by Standard & Poor's, Moody's, or Duff & Phelps.
- Consider giving money to your loved ones. Even after you've left $625,000 to your heirs estate-tax-free, you and your spouse still have room to navigate. One avenue is to give away up to $10,000 per parent per person annually while you're still alive to cut the size of your taxable estate. But watch out. If you give away more than $10,000 annually, you could be subject to federal gift tax.

You might want to evaluate carefully how you give this money away. Here's a rundown:

- With cash. You can give away money to your children, relatives, friends, or charity. But you have no control over the money once you give it away. So your children can do whatever they want with it.
- Tuition and medical care. Tax laws permit you to give an unlimited amount, provided it is for your child's or grandchild's tuition and medical care. You have to make payments directly to the school or doctor.
- Minor accounts. If you prefer to keep control of the money until your child is an adult, but simultaneously reduce the size of your taxable estate, you can use the Uniform Gift to Minors Act (UGMA). You put money into a custodial account for your child, but when the child turns 18 or the age of majority in your state, it's all his or hers.
- Charitable remainder trust. You set up an irrevocable trust fund with a charity. The charity pays you income for life. When you die, the money goes to the charity.

- Charitable lead trust. The charity receives the investment income while you are alive, but assets in the trust go to the beneficiaries when you die.

Ten Steps to Estate Planning

1. Take your financial inventory. Figure your net worth or your total assets less your total liabilities.
2. Meet with an experienced accountant, financial planner, and attorney to help you set up an estate game plan.
3. Review your financial goals. Make sure you're saving for retirement and have adequate life insurance and disability insurance coverage.
4. Decide who should inherit your money and property when you die. Ask yourself how much you want to leave your spouse, children, relatives, or friends.
5. Determine the cost of probating a will versus establishing a revocable or irrevocable living trust.
6. Review the tax ramifications. Estimate how much your estate will be worth by the time you die.
7. Look into ways you can cut the size of your taxable estate.
8. Make provisions to pay any estate taxes due. You might not think you'll owe estate taxes, but over time, your assets could grow to more than you think.
9. Evaluate the cost of life insurance that can be use to pay estate taxes.

☞ Hot Tip • • •

If you leave all your property to your spouse, you escape the tax man. Eventually, however, estate taxes must be paid when the second spouse dies. Financial planners stress that anyone with an estate exceeding $625,000 should consider setting up a life insurance irrevocable trust. The life insurance proceeds in the trust escape estate taxation, plus the death benefits can be used to pay the estate-tax bill.

• • • • •

10. If you set up a trust, make sure that it is valid. A trust agreement should include the following items: how the trust is managed and how the assets should be distributed; identification of the property in the trust; names of beneficiaries (those who will receive your assets); name of a trustee to manage the trust assets; and terms of when the trust will end.

Managing
Your Money

You've come a long way together! But the money in your marriage—or lack of it—and the emotional upheavals it triggers never seem to end. This section shows you how to make the right money moves when you buy a house, have children, and save for their college education. Plan ahead for these milestones, and you'll both have happier and healthier lives together. In this section, you'll also learn how to be well-prepared financially just in case you suffer through any of life's traumas, such as putting a spouse in a nursing home, burying the person you love most, or—dare we say it—divorce. Assuming, though, that you can avoid some of this pain and suffering, perhaps partially through some good financial planning early on, there's good news on the horizon. You've made it this far together. Now—with just a little help from your friends—retirement should be a breeze!

Chapter 12

Feathering Your Nest: Your Place, Mine, or Ours

When you live together or get married, there are a lot of decisions to make about your home. Should you live in your partner's home, your home, or buy a new place altogether? Should you rent rather than own? If it's an entirely new place you're considering, you then have to agree on a decor as well as how much to spend on your abode and its furnishings—not to mention who's invited to visit and when. This chapter discusses some of the decisions you'll need to make concerning where you live, ideas on how to cut costs, and pointers on how to agree on all the home-related decisions you'll face.

If One Spouse Already Owns Property

It may be good news if one of you already owns property. You get to save money. You may not have to go out and buy furniture. At least one of you does not need to radically change a lifestyle.

But there may be ghosts lurking in your partner's bedroom that can haunt you if you let them. You might feel uncomfortable moving into a place that was paid for by someone else. A spouse who owns the property might harbor some hidden resentment to a spouse who didn't help foot the bills.

There also may be questions lurking in the back of your mind about your new partner's ex-spouse or lovers that make it difficult for you to sleep in the same bedroom.

Don't forget. Both of you already may be carrying around a lot of excess baggage from your previous relationships. If you don't discuss these feelings openly, you might run into problems—and not just financial ones either.

There are several things the one moving in can do to help himself or herself feel better.

On the money side, if you're feeling uncomfortable because you're not footing the bills, you might contribute your half of the downpayment for the mortgage to your new partner. Or you could put up more money when the house is refinanced. Buy new things for the house. Or open a new investment account in both your names with your own money.

Gail: Al, why are you hanging up your Willie Mays framed autograph in the living room?

Al: I was getting a little tired of the color mauve.

However, creating a financial balance might not work if you can't sleep at night because of ex-lovers that have preceded you. Consider changing rooms. Psychologists say don't just shrug these feelings off. If you're uncomfortable now, just wait!

As far as the law is concerned, any spouse moving in may have a full-fledged right to some emotional insecurities. In a majority of states, a home may be considered separate property if the title never was changed—particularly if one spouse never contributed to it financially.

Should You Rent or Own?

Take some time with this one folks. If you're buying your first home together, be ready to shell out big bucks. Can you afford it?

As we mentioned earlier, the two of you, we suspect, have different money backgrounds. Based on your previous experience growing up, for example, one of you might want to avoid a mortgage. Perhaps your spouse's relative experienced a foreclosure on a home. Or maybe there were feelings of resentment by one set of parents for having been a slave to a mortgage.

On the other hand, perhaps a home was a source of pleasure to one of you growing up, and socializing in your abode meant fun times you'd like to rekindle.

Of course, there also may be personal feelings. A home to one of you might represent old age, settling down, a slower-paced life that you'd like to avoid. For the other, it might mean security and a happy family life. These are some initial issues you may have to compromise on.

It's true. When you rent, you have no responsibility for the upkeep of a house or condo. You don't have to come up with a big down payment or pay for ongoing repairs—although often who pays for repairs is a matter of nego-

! H O W   T O   C O M M U N I C A T E
. . . . .

1. Tell your partner exactly how you feel about buying a home versus renting. Elicit his or her feelings.

2. Appreciate your partner's feelings, and tell him or her of your appreciation.

3. Brainstorm ways you can meet each other in the middle; i.e., if one of you gets sick at the thought of living in the suburbs, perhaps you can find a section of the city that has a pretty park. Or maybe you can agree to spend weekends in the city, while maintaining a home in the suburbs.

4. Mentally acknowledge how you feel about any compromise.

5. Reward yourselves for reaching an agreement. Crack open a bottle of champagne!

. . . . .

tiation. You can leave after your one-year lease is up—assuming you have a lease. You have flexibility. If you have to pick up and move, you generally can do it more easily than you could if you owned the home.

Buying a house is a lot more responsibility. But there are a lot of advantages. When you buy, there's some hope that, at least eventually, you'll be paying less than you would if you rent. That's assuming inflation continues at its historic pace of about 3 percent annually. Plus you are putting money into an asset. Later on, you can sell your home at a profit—provided that real estate prices have risen. You get nothing but a bunch of receipts when you pay rent.

Beaucoup Tax Breaks

While there are numerous financial benefits to buying a home, perhaps the greatest is the tax deductibility of the mortgage interest, up-front points, and property taxes. Initially, it might not feel like you're getting a bigger bargain by buying a home compared with renting. But chances are you'll be heaving a sigh of relief when it comes time to pay Uncle Sam—particularly if you're in a high tax bracket. It's not uncommon to save hundreds or even thousands of dollars annually due to home-related tax deductions. But this is something for you to confirm with your accountant.

To see how the tax benefits could work, let's look at the Smiths. They just bought a three-bedroom home for $98,800. It is slightly larger than the three-bedroom apartment they previously rented for $900 per month. The following shows a breakdown of this family's new monthly mortgage payment. Once the tax deduction of mortgage interest and property taxes is factored in, the "real" mortgage payment winds up being less than the amount they were paying in rent.

The Smiths put 10 percent down on a $98,800 house. They have a $88,920 mortgage for 30 years at a fixed rate of $7^{1}/_{4}$ percent. The monthly mortgage payment is $868.59.

Your Home Can Appreciate in Value, Too

In most regions, home values generally rise, or "appreciate," in response to local and economic trends—usually at a pace that meets or beats inflation. Historically, real estate has appreciated in value at about 3 percent more than

Figure 12.1 Tax Savings	
Mortgage for the Smith's home	$868.59
Principal and interest	606.59
Property tax	206.00
Homeowners insurance	23.00
Mortgage insurance	33.00
Tax deduction at 28 percent bracket	206.00
Real monthly mortgage costs—Mortgage less tax deduction	662.59

Who benefits from the $206 a month in tax savings? The Smiths. If they rented, they wouldn't get this kind of break. When the Smiths added things up over the year and factored in the tax deduction, they really benefited from owning the house rather than paying $900 per month in rent. Of course, if you're in a lower tax bracket, the benefits may not necessarily be as great.

the inflation rate. This means when you sell your house, you may be able to sell it for more than you paid for it, and pocket a nice piece of change. You can't exactly make money like this from renting.

In addition to appreciation, other factors enhance the investment in your new home. As the years go by, you begin to pay off more and more of the loan's principal with each monthly mortgage payment. This, along with appreciation and your original down payment, builds "equity," which translates into cash when you decide to sell your home. You can use this smart automatic savings for a number of purposes—to buy a bigger home, for your children's college education, as collateral for a home equity loan, or to have a rent-free abode in your retirement.

When you put money into a home, you make an investment in your future. By contrast, each time you send in a rental check, you build the land-lord's equity—and never see your money again.

Does home ownership seem right for you? Your first step is to determine the price range your income will support. The general rule of thumb is that you can afford a home that costs up to $2\frac{1}{2}$ times your annual income before taxes—including the down payment.

But with all the job downsizings in recent years, we probably would advise spending less. It's not worth the stress! It's also a good idea to put 20 percent down on your home. By coming up with 20 percent down, you'll avoid having to pay extra for private mortgage insurance (PMI). Plus, your payments will be a little lower than if you put down less.

Going Shopping: How to Deal with a Real Estate Agent

Even though you may hook up with a real estate agent, it's important to do your own homework. If your agent is a member of the National Association of Realtors®, he or she is required to abide by a certain code of ethics. But keep in mind that all agents, no matter who they represent, have one objective: making a sale.

Chances are your agent probably will give you a "disclosure agreement" to sign indicating who he or she represents. Most agents represent the seller, and aggressively are working on the seller's behalf. This is important to know because you won't want to tip your hand on your negotiation strategies in front of a "seller's agent." Someone who works for you, a "buyer's agent," will negotiate on your behalf and shop more aggressively for a home and terms to meet your needs. Nevertheless, even if your broker's agent does represent you—the buyer–chances are that the agent will collect a commission from the seller anyway, and still will be anxious to close the sale. With a "dual agent," the agent represents both parties. This arrangement is illegal in some states, and could lead to conflicts of interest. Meanwhile, "transaction agents," who represent neither party, are growing in popularity. The transaction agent's sole purpose is to make the sale happen. So don't get the wrong idea that the agent is working on your behalf. Regardless of where your agent's loyalties lie, you need to look after your own interests.

Our advice is that regardless of whether you use an agent or go it on your own, always take the following steps:

- Check the location of the property, including schools. The quality of schools in an area often affects property values and how much they appreciate.

- Inspect a potential home carefully in daylight. You'll see imperfections a little better this way. Bring a notepad and jot down improvements you have to make. Look for peeled or cracked paint, check faucets for leaks, and, if possible, talk to neighbors to see if there are any unusual problems with the property.

- If you're using a real estate agent, ask for a comparative marketing analysis (CMA report), which gives the actual sale price of similar homes in the neighborhood. Figure out the median price in the area. This gives you a starting point for negotiation. Then you can offer more or less based on the owner's situation and how badly you want the property. Not using an agent? Often, you can check the sale prices of nearby homes via a phone call to the county property appraiser's office.

- Ask how long a house has been up for sale. Also note whether it is empty. An owner might be more eager to sell an empty home that requires monthly mortgage payments to continue.

- Learn whether the seller is carrying a mortgage—information that should be available from the county clerk. It stands to reason that an anxious seller with no mortgage might be more willing to take a lower price than a seller who is forced to pay off a mortgage first.

- Put in phone calls to the area's planning board and, if applicable, the homeowners' or condo association. You want to know about the zoning of property surrounding your purchase. If a neighboring lot is zoned industrial, for example, the value might not appreciate quite as fast as you'd hope. You'll also want to ask whether any major construction projects that could influence the home's value are being considered.

- Is there a homeowner's or condo association? You'll want to check whether any special assessments are in the works. Plus, you'll want to know about any litigation against the association that could affect the value of the home or condo. You'll need to make certain the association is well-run by reviewing its financial statement, and you'll want a chance to review bylaws to make sure you can live with them.

Nailing Down a Mortgage

It's always best to be prequalified first by a reputable lender, and determine whether you feel comfortable with the resulting monthly payments. Check newspapers for lenders offering low rates in your area. You can check mortgage rates on the Internet at Bank Rate Monitor—www.bankrate.com.

Once you've found a few lenders offering attractive rates, ask them for a "good faith estimate," which should give you an idea of monthly payments and list the other costs involved. You

> **☞ Hot Tip • • •**
>
> **O**ften, you can save money by buying a resale rather than a new home. Of course, the savings you realize by purchasing a resale only are worth it if you don't have to spend it all on repairs. On the other hand, with a new home, you're apt to have a warranty on repairs.
>
> • • • • •

then can see whether you feel comfortable with the costs and compare various offers. You want to go with the lowest-cost lender who will qualify you for the type of mortgage you want. If you already have a checking account or other banking relationship with a lender who seems to be offering a pretty good deal, you might be able to do even better. Some lenders are willing to knock a quarter-point or so off your loan rate or cut your fees if you're already a customer.

It's always a good idea to first check with local Better Business Bureau and appropriate regulatory agency to make certain there are no unresolved complaints filed against the lender you're considering. There's nothing worse than being ready to close on the home of your dreams and the lender is not ready.

The most common type of mortgage is a 30-year fixed-rate mortgage, in which your rate doesn't change for the full 30 years. These mortgages generally are a good idea if you think you're going to be in your home a long time.

With adjustable-rate mortgages (ARMs), the rate is subject to change. How frequently the rate changes depends upon the type of mortgage. ARMs may be a better deal if you don't think you'll be in your home very long. That's because there's less chance your rate can go up. Before selecting an adjustable-rate mortgage, you'll want to examine how high your monthly payment can go based on your "life-of-loan" cap. Then, see how comfortable you feel if the rate hits that level. Always examine the caps—how high the rate can go, and floors—how low the rate can go, very carefully.

Consult a Lawyer

It's important to consult with a lawyer in drawing up your contract to avoid missing any important items.

"Some buyers don't know that they have to apply for financing within a certain number of days," warns Jeffrey S. Raynor, a Florida-certified real estate lawyer who practices in Juno Beach. "Some don't understand that if they don't get financing and they don't cancel the contract, they may have waived the financing contingency inadvertently." In such a case, Raynor says, the buyer could wind up having to come up with cash for the sale.

It's critical, Raynor says, to make certain that your initial deposit is placed in a third-party "escrow account." "It's much easier to get your money back

☞ Hot Tip • • •

Beware of mortgages that have "payment caps," which limit increases in your monthly payments rather than rate caps. You could get hit big-time if rates head up quickly. Even though your payment increase is limited, you could wind up owing more than the house originally cost, due to rate increases, if you're not careful. This is a phenomenon is known as "negative amortization."

Also, watch out for balloon loans. You'll have very small monthly payments, almost all interest, for a specific period of time—say seven years. Then, at the end of the term, the full amount of your loan comes due. Balloon loans may be attractive if you know you're going to be in your home a short period of time and if homes are appreciating. If not, you could be stuck paying off your full sale price or forced to refinance at a higher rate.

• • • • •

from a third-party if there's a default," he said.

"Some people don't do inspections, even though they have the right to do so," he adds. You'll want to be certain that whatever deal you agree upon is contingent upon a thorough inspection, qualifying for a mortgage you can afford, and review of any homeowner's association documents and that association's approval, if required.

> **☞ Hot Tip • • •**
>
> **F**or a list of members of the American Society of Home Inspectors in your area, you can call 800-743-2744. It's a good idea to be present during the inspection so you can determine how serious the problems are.
>
> • • • • •

Thorough inspections, which typically run from $200 to $500, should include the structure, roof, appliances, and pests. Be certain to locate a reputable inspector—preferably one not recommended by the seller's agent, who has the ulterior motive of making a sale and collecting a commission from the seller.

Should You Own Your Home Jointly or in One Name?

As we indicated earlier in this chapter, this issue can be particularly touchy. A home represents a source of security to many people. If you're not careful, one of you inadvertently may experience resentment if the title is in one of your names and not the other's. The longer you're married, the more this resentment can build. Better to discuss these feelings up front, before you make the decision.

Who holds title to a property also can govern how much you pay in taxes, and who gets the property when you die. For example if you have children from a previous marriage, you may not want to own the property jointly with your spouse. Also, there may be certain tax advantages to owning property separately.

Fortunately, regardless of who owns the property, there are some key tax benefits of home ownership. Chief among them: Thanks to the Taxpayer Relief Act of 1997, you might not have to worry about capital gains taxes on the sale of your main residence. For home sales after May 7, 1997, married couples pay no tax on the first $500,000 of capital gain from the sale of a principal residence. Singles are exempt on $250,000. To be eligible for this tax break, the home must have been your principal residence for at least two of the five years prior to the sale. This exemption can be used once every two years.

What if you sold a home before May 7, 1997?

You can postpone the capital gains tax on the sale of your home if you buy and live in another home at least of equal value within two years before or after the sale. Say you're under 55, you sell the house you purchased for $100,000 for $150,000, pocketing $50,000, and immediately buy a smaller home for $95,000. You'd have to pay 28 percent capital gains tax on the $50,000 profit or $14,000. But if you buy a house for more than $100,000, you pay no capital gains tax.

Also under the old law, if you're at least 55 years old, you get a one-time $125,000 capital gains exclusion on the sale of your primary home at a profit.

Now for the hard part: determining whose name to put your home in. You should know that in general, most married couples typically opt for "joint tenancy with right of survivorship" as the way to hold title to a home. This means, you both own the home equally. If one of you dies it automatically reverts to the other regardless of whether you have a will. As we discussed in Chapter 7, there may be tax advantages to owning a home or other types of property in one person's name. It's best to consult your financial adviser on this issue.

Can you write off a loss on your home? No way, Jose!

IRS rules dealing with marriage and owning a home are a strange breed. IRS publication 523 covers the topic.

Congratulations, You're Expecting...

Now you're in for the most radical change in your lives since you tied the knot! Preparing for your cute little bundle of joy. Anytime a new person enters or leaves your life, it's a time of stress in a marriage. But make certain you're financially prepared for this blessed event, and it sure will help smooth the way.

Preparing for Your Little Tax Benefit

Fortunately, this is a happy occasion. But logistically and financially, it requires much planning. Nowadays, many of you may be two-paycheck couples.

We hate to break it to you, but the U.S. Department of Agriculture estimates that middle-income parents are likely to spend more than a whopping $9,000 in the child's first year alone. By the time the child reaches 18, the total cost will be nearly $300,000.

Don't be discouraged. The downside if you wait too long is you'll never have children and miss one of the greatest joys of life. Just start off with a little planning, and you'll be further along than many couples.

First you'll want to evaluate your health insurance situation. Insurers typically require that you buy pregnancy coverage at least three months before your pregnancy starts. Whether or not you have insurance, you'll want to establish how much you'll be required to shell out for this blessed event, and start saving early. The federal government pegs unreimbursed medical bills for the obstetrician and hospital alone to be $1,200.

If you use a hospital, investigate how room rates are charged. You might be able to save on the price of a room, for example, if you arrive at night and leave at mid-day.

In the meantime, you have at least a little protection. The Hills-Burton Act requires a hospital to accept people who are undergoing an emergency condition regardless of whether they have insurance. While pregnancy might not be considered an emergency, labor certainly is.

☞ *Hot Tip* • • •

Best to avoid telling everybody and his or her brother that the two of you are expecting until after the first three months that you're pregnant. It's during those early stages that most miscarriages occur. Besides, you might want to use that period to investigate what pregnancy benefits are available.

• • • • •

Bet You
Didn't Know

• • • • •

Don't have insurance? The average cost of delivery runs about $3,000, but there are some other options if you don't anticipate medical complications.

More hospitals are offering short-term care packages in which they keep you only overnight and send you home with a nurse.

Many states now have licensed birthing centers, staffed by certified nurse-midwives and consulting physicians on a 24-hour basis. But there is one important drawback. They lack operating rooms and intensive care centers—critical facilities in the event of complications.

Home birth is another option. Nurse-midwives today are state-licensed and, like registered nurses, you can find names in the yellow pages. But it is critical that you obtain references first, and that you only go this route if you're pretty certain your birth won't be complicated.

• • • • •

Figure
13.1

• • • • •
New Baby Checklist

Hospital:
Hospital bills   _____
Doctor bills   _____

Baby:
Clothes   _____
Blankets   _____
Disposable diapers   _____
Booties and socks   _____

Nursery:
Sheets   _____
Waterproof pads   _____
Blankets   _____
Crib and mattress   _____
Bassinet   _____
Portable baby seat   _____
Baby carriage   _____
Feeding equipment   _____
Bath items   _____
Miscellaneous   _____

Do you both plan to work after the birth of a child? Figure at least $7,000 per year for day care.

Plus, you'll need a basic wardrobe for the baby. Check to see if you can wangle any hand-me-downs from friends or family members. You'll also need nursery items such as bathing equipment.

Don't forget maternity clothes.

Next, you need to determine how much leave you'll need from your job, or if you'll be returning at all. Luckily, the Family and Medical Leave Act of 1993 requires employers to offer workers 12 weeks of unpaid leave with continuation of health benefits to both men and women in the case of a pregnancy.

Plus, the Federal Pregnancy Discrimination Act prohibits an employer with at least 15 employees from reassigning you, forcing you to take a leave, or refusing to hire you back because you are pregnant. If you become temporarily unable to work because of pregnancy, your employer must treat you the same as any other temporarily disabled employee. In addition, most states have leave laws of their own.

Should Dad consider a paternity leave? You don't see Dad taking family leave very often. However it's happening more frequently. If you're a loyal employee, consider talking it over with

Bet You Didn't Know
• • • • •

For information on the federal leave law, contact the nearest U.S. Department of Labor Wage and Hour Division.

For information on the Pregnancy Discrimination Act, contact your nearest Equal Employment Opportunity Commission, 800-669-4000.

For information on your state's laws, contact the state's labor department or commission on civil or human rights.

• • • • •

! How to Communicate
• • • • •

First determine exactly how much work you'll each be willing to miss. Discuss the following issues:

- Exactly how much unpaid leave can you afford? Many experts recommend at least three to five months' leave to allow bonding with the baby.
- Whether Mom would like to go back to work.
- Whether Dad should take off too.
- What arrangements you'll make for childcare.

• • • • •

your boss. If your wife has to get back to work to help pay the bills, you can split your family leave time. If money is tight, Dad might consider taking the leave after Mom returns to work so that less money need be spent on childcare.

Of course, all these laws may be well and good, but many parents can't afford to take off without pay. Also, many of you may not be covered by the family leave law, which requires your employer to have at least 50 employees. And, you must have worked at least 1,250 hours in the past year.

A big issue with many families is whether Mom should go back to work at all. If you're like most people, you may need the extra income. But if at all possible, it's best for Mom to stay home with the baby for at least a year. That's a critical

---

☞ *Hot Tip* • • •

If you expect to be returning to work, determine from your personnel office or supervisor exactly what benefits you'll receive.

Once you've figured out exactly what you hope to achieve in the way of paid leave, then you can talk to your boss. Try not to agree to take a lower salary in exchange for working at home. You'll want to know about your job protection, whether you'll still have health insurance benefits, and if your company sponsors aprenatal class and offers time off for it, Also, does your employer provide childcare or offer childcare assistance?

• • • • •

Figure 13.2 • • • • •
Pregnancy Checklist

With your new arrival you'll want to consider:

- Adding more life insurance
- Changing your health insurance to add your child
- Revising your budget to include your child
- Reviewing disability insurance
- Revising your wills
- Appointing guardians for your child

time when the baby needs nurturing by a loving mother. See Chapter 5, Figure 5.1, Should You Return to Work?

Although your expenses are likely to increase once your bundle of joy arrives, Uncle Sam has a little gift waiting in the wings. You now get to claim your child as a dependent, which qualifies you for an extra income tax exemption—$2,650 in 1997. This exemption, though, gets phased out over certain income levels.

In 1998 and beyond, parents will get a tax credit that's a dollar-for-dollar reduction in the tax you pay of $400 per child age 16 or under. The credit will be $500 in 1999. But these credits are phased out with adjusted gross income of more than $110,000 for couples, $75,000 for singles.

The other advantage your little newcomer brings is that any of your child's earnings up to $650 are exempt from federal taxes, and the next $650 is taxed only at the child's tax rate, 15 percent in 1997. So if both parents are in a high tax bracket, you can file a separate tax return for junior, and save a few bucks.

Arranging for Childcare

Talk about being put in a bind. It can cost you $150 a week or more to put your child in a day care center. But if you must go back to work, you don't have much choice.

You might consider hiring a "doula" to visit the home for two to four hours a day for two to three weeks to help with child care and light housekeeping. Costs vary, but the average ranges about $25 an hour. Some hospitals supply this service, although it rarely is covered by health insurance. To find out about doulas in your area, contact the National Association of

Bet You Didn't Know

• • • • •

You needn't worry about putting your children in day care, according to the latest research.

A federally funded study, which tracked 1,300 children from birth to age three, indicates children's speech and intellectual development are not hindered by day care. The family's household environment carries more weight in the child's development than what happens while in childcare, according to a study sponsored by the National Institute of Child Health and Human Development.

• • • • •

Postpartum Care Services, 326 Shields St., San Francisco, California 94132-2734 (206-672-8011).

Other options are baby nurses who solely take care of the baby.

Before you do anything, check with your employer to see if there are any day care benefits. More companies have "flexible spending accounts," by which employees can exempt up to $5,000 from federal, and often state, taxes.

Home-based care is another option. You don't have to bother picking your child up at day care or missing work when your child is ill. Your child won't be exposed to as many germs, and you might even be able to get your caregiver to do some housework. It's particularly advantageous if you have more than one child.

But unless you have a friend or relative supplying this service, you're likely to pay more than you will for group day care. When the caregiver is sick, you're out of luck. Also, when you're not around, particularly if the child can't talk, you don't know what's going on. Turnover often is high with home-based care—a point that can disappoint your child or make things harder for the next caregiver.

Meanwhile, if it's a live-in you've chosen, you're giving up some privacy. You'll want to first determine which qualities are important to you. You can hire an older person with years of experience. You'll have a mature person looking after your child. Or you might opt for a younger, more energetic person. The person's religion and political views also may be important.

Among the options you might consider:

- Nannies. These caregivers have had some formal childcare training and typically demand higher pay. You can get a list of nanny schools from the American Council of Nanny Schools, Delta College, University Center, MI 48710 (517-686-9417).
- Au pairs. These generally are younger people, often from another country, who live in as part of a type of foreign exchange program. To get the official list of au pairs, call the U.S. Information Agency, 202-475-2389.
- Babysitters. All others whose training comes from personal experience.

You might consider running an ad for whichever you've decided upon. You also can check with friends, pediatricians, area colleges, or local religious institutions.

Once the child is ready for day care, you can expect to spend anywhere from $300 to $600 monthly.

Unable to be there as much as you'd like?

For young children, there should be a low-care-giver-to-child ratio at the day care center. While under seven-to-one is considered good, two-or three-to-one is even better.

Other things to check:

☞ Hot Tip • • •

Once you hire someone to care for your child, check to see whether you are subject to federal and/or state laws or taxes. Upon interviewing the candidates, it's a good idea to provide them with a job description, including a starting date; salary, including overtime; and hours, including whether the job will involve staying late and working weekends or holidays. Also include a list of benefits.

• • • • •

- Does the staff have training in infant cardiopulmonary resuscitation?
- What qualifications does the staff have?
- Are parents welcome to drop in at any time?
- How are the staff screened?
- Does the facility have all required state licenses?
- How clean is it?
- What is the staff turnover rate?
- How often are diapers changed?
- How healthy is the food served?
- What kinds of activities are the kids participating in?
- How does the child spend time in the facility?

You might check with the agency that regulates day care centers in your state to see if any complaints have been filed against a facility you're considering. Also, make an on-site visit to see firsthand how children are treated and whether play areas are safe.

Saving for the Little One's Higher Education

It's tough enough to meet your everyday living expenses. Meanwhile, staring you straight in the face is a double whammy—saving for a child's higher education and your own retirement.

Unless you're lucky enough to be born into wealth, or you just happen to pick the right numbers in the lottery, there's only one other way to meet these challenges: save, save, save! Make the wrong investment decisions, or shun the idea of investing altogether, and you could wind up short-funded.

Get Ready to Shell Out Some Big Bucks

You've probably already heard the stories. College expenses could double in ten years. Four years of public university now costs about $38,000. Private colleges may cost twice that much. By the time your newborn is ready for a higher education, assuming costs rise 7 percent annually, four years at a public college could cost almost $120,000.

Figure 13.3 • • • • •

What It Costs for College

Assume college costs are rising 7 percent annually and your investments earn 8 percent annually. To see how much you need to save to send each child to college, look at the following table:

Year Beginning	Public College	Monthly Savings	Private College	Monthly Savings
2000	$65,000	$885	$130,000	$1,770
2005	91,000	498	182,000	995
2010	119,000	344	234,000	677

All this means you need to save $344 a month over the next 15 years to cover the full cost of a future college education, assuming you can earn 8 percent annually.

Suppose your little Einstein wants to be a Harvard man or woman and attend another Ivy League school? Then, you'll have to save $677 a month at 8 percent to pay for an estimated $238,000 for four years.

Some tax credits to help your savings plan will be discussed in the next section.

How Much Do You Need to Save?

All this might sound a little intimidating, but actually it involves a planning. It might not be a bad idea to talk to a financial planner to help you get on a budget and savings plan. It takes some doing to save for retirement as well as college. But don't get scared. Just start saving whatever you can. The rest will take care of itself. Keep in mind it's easier to get college financing today than ever before.

Financial planners suggest saving to pay for at least half the cost. The balance can be financed through college financial aid and scholarships and student loans from good old Uncle Sam.

Other sources: bank loans, home equity loans, and life insurance loans against cash value policies. Don't forget your child may receive a scholarship. Frequently, grandparents give money to children for college. It also helps if your teenager works part-time and contributes to the education kitty.

Sure, you say. Today you can finance 100 percent of the cost of college by getting government loans. True, the Clinton administration passed laws a couple of years ago so that everyone could afford a higher education. Government loans to consider include Perkins, Stafford and Pell Grants, and Plus Loans.

You can deduct student loan interest, which was being phased in to $2,500 per year for the first five years of repayment. You can get a maximum $1,500 Hope Scholarship tax credit in the child's freshman and sophomore years for a child who spent at least $2,000. The credit works this way. You get to credit up to 100 percent of a child's educational costs to $1,000, 50 percent for the next $1,000 in costs.

In the child's junior and senior year, though, credits shrink. A Lifetime Learning tax credit, available to students in degree and nondegree programs, is capped at $1,000 annually, increasing to $2,000 annually in the year 2003.

The Lifetime Learning credit is calculated at 20 percent of your educational expenses up to $5,000, $10,000 beginning in the year 2003. All credits are phased out for joint filers with adjusted gross income starting at $80,000 and for single taxpayers with adjusted gross incomes starting at $40,000. Parents are prohibited from taking both the Hope credit and the Lifetime Learning credit in one year.

You also can get a tax deduction for your contribution into a prepaid tuition plan, as long as your child goes to a public institution.

One more big break: The Taxpayer Relief Act of 1997 permits parents to make nondeductible contributions of $500 per year per child under 18 into an educational IRA. The funds can be withdrawn for higher educational expenses tax free.

> ☞ *Hot Tip* • • •
>
> **B**orrow all the money for your child's education and you or your child could be saddled with too much debt when he or she graduates.
>
> • • • • •

How to Invest

Once you've got a fix on how much you need for college, you can invest to reach your goal. As discussed in earlier chapters, the longer you have, the more you should invest in stock funds.

One thing you don't need when you're investing for your child's college education is more taxes! There are a couple of ways, besides investing in tax-free bond funds or money funds, to reduce the tax bite of saving for your child. Probably the easiest and most common method simply is to put the investment in the child's name.

> ☞ *Hot Tip* • • •
>
> **S**pecial college savings plans offered by Fidelity Investments (800-544-8888) and American Century (800-345-2021) dollar cost average into a stock fund. Money automatically is moved into the fixed-income fund of your choice when your child nears college age.
>
> • • • • •

Figure
13.4

Mutual Fund Investments to Save for College

Type of Fund	Child's Age	Risk

**Aggressive or
Growth Funds** 1-12 **High**

Comments: These funds invest in growth stocks. You can expect to average 10 to 12 percent per year, earning between -11 percent and +31 percent per year (a typical range). After age 12, substitute growth and income or balanced funds.

**High Yield
Bond Funds** 1-8 **High**

Comments: Yields may be above 10 percent, but risky. Put only a small portion of college savings in this type of fund. Interest rate and credit risk. Parents in high tax brackets can consider municipal bond funds. (See Chapter 10, page 167.)

**Zero Coupon
T-Bond Funds** 1-15 **Moderate**

Comments: Bond funds own T-bonds that pay principal and interest at maturity. So you know how much you will have when college starts. Yields 6 to 7 percent.

**High Grade Corporate
Bond Funds** 1-18 **Moderate**

Comments: Funds invest in A to AAA-rated bonds. Current yield 7 percent. Interest rate risk. Parents in high tax brackets can consider municipal bond funds.

**Short-Term
Bond Funds** 1-18 **Low**

Comments: Funds invest in U.S. Treasury and corporate bonds. Less risky than long-term bonds, but yield up to 6 percent. Parents in high tax brackets can consider municipal bond funds.

Money Funds 1-18 **Low**

Comments: Funds invest in short-term money market instruments. Yields 5 percent today. Parents in high tax brackets can consider tax-free money funds.

It's generally best to set up a custodial account with a financial institution using the Uniform Gift to Minors Act (UGMA) or the Uniform Transfer to Minors Act (UTMA). Grandparents also may give the child money for college using this tactic. The IRS allows an annual gift of $10,000 per adult without charging gift taxes. However, if you take this route, the money becomes the child's when he or she turns 18, or whatever age your state considers adulthood. EE U.S Savings Bonds are another option. When you cash out the EE bonds, you might avoid paying taxes on earnings if you use the proceeds to pay for your child's tuition. These tax breaks partially are phased out, though, with annual adjusted gross incomes of more than $66,200, and they're fully phased out when adjusted gross income reaches $96,200.

EE bonds pay rates that are adjusted twice a year, based on Treasury security yields. You can invest as little as $25 for a $50 savings bond and as much as $15,000 for a $30,000 savings bond in any year.

Bet You Didn't Know
• • • • •

There are several free sources of information on saving for college that may help you get started. They include:

• 12 Tips for College Savers, Neuberger & Berman Management, Inc., 800-877-9700.
• Federal Student Aid Information Center fields your questions at 800-333-INFO.
• *Paying For College: A Step-by-Step College Planning Guide*, T. Rowe Price Investment Services, 800-225-5135.
• The College Board, a nonprofit association, also has a number of publications that are helpful. Call 800-323-7155 for more information.

• • • • •

When the Road Gets Rocky

This chapter deals with everybody's greatest fears when it comes to tying the knot or getting in a deep commitment with the opposite sex: things might not work out. Or illness or death can strike at any time. But separation at some point from the love of your life does happen. The emotional upheaval may be slightly less traumatic if you can remove some of the financial strains involved.

A Word about Divorce

We hope that many of the pointers we've given you about money, which in some cases, also may apply to other areas of your married life, will help you avoid this section of this chapter.

The married people we know seem a lot happier than those who are divorced. Both are working and enjoy a higher standard of living than our single friends. Our remarried friends seem a lot happier the second time around.

It takes a couple of years to get over the emotional trauma of a divorce. Plus, once you've split, your standard of living may deteriorate.

Women seem to be the hardest hit. We have divorced friends who have to raise the kids on just their income. Child support or alimony helps a little. But it's a big expense when you consider food, clothing, medical expenses, and getting children off to college.

It's easy to see why four out of every ten divorced women say they experienced financially tougher times after they divorced, according to a survey conducted by the National Survey of Families and Households.

Plus, divorce is pretty tough on kids. Nevertheless, half of all marriages are ending in divorce. If you feel compelled to join this crew, better to be prepared for the emotional and financial repercussions. It's been estimated that it takes two to four years to recuperate emotionally from a divorce, during which time, many people become more self-centered and may withdraw from the rest of their families.

Serious about a divorce? There are a lot of issues you have to deal with, like who will have custody of the kids and where you and your spouse will live.

Contrary to popular belief, divorce lawyers note that the courts don't favor the woman over the man when it comes to custody of the children. The decision is based on the child's best interests. Regardless of who the child stays with, the other parent usually can visit.

To obtain a divorce, you need to learn about all your spouse's assets. Yes, there are do-it-yourself kits around that can help cut your costs if you're both on good terms. Even so, you'll each want your own lawyers to review the settlement. There are just too many issues involved.

Each of you will need copies of all records such as tax returns, payroll stubs, pensions, property appraisals, deeds, bank statements, credit card state-

> ### Bet You Didn't Know
>
> • • • • •
>
> It could get harder to divorce if more states follow Louisiana's pilot example of an optional "covenant marriage." Couples choosing a covenant marriage can only divorce via reasons such as adultery, abuse, abandonment, or lengthy separation.
>
> • • • • •

> ### ☞ Hot Tip • • •
>
> Unsure about a divorce? Many couples get a "legal separation" from the courts. Sometimes after a cooling off period, people get back together, particularly if they obtain psychological counseling.
>
> • • • • •

ments, investments, insurance policies, and credit records. If you own a business, its value must be assessed.

Don't forget debts. Unfortunately, a divorce does not relieve either of you from those if you've jointly signed on the loans or credit cards.

However, if you suspect your spouse might run up more debt and hold you liable, you should notify the lender in writing that you will not be responsi-

> ☞ *Hot Tip* • • •
>
> **Y**ou might be able to save money by going to a mediator instead of going to lawyers. Mediators will sit the parties down and hash out an agreement about who gets what.
>
> • • • • •

ble for any more debts on the joint account beyond the current outstanding balance.

Once you've got the divorce ball rolling, you have to move money, investments, valuables, and property into your own account. Notify your financial advisers that you're getting a divorce. Be sure to change beneficiaries on retirement plans, wills, and insurance policies.

Lawyers advise that you destroy any power of attorney that gives your spouse control over your assets or health, and notify your bank and broker in writing not to accept any copies.

In most states you will have to wait at least six months before your divorce can be finalized. The person seeking the divorce will have to state the reasons for divorce in papers filed with the court, although all states now permit no-fault divorces, except for covenant marriages.

Once you and your lawyers have looked at all the money and property you've amassed over the years, you'll both agree on a "marital settlement agreement," detailing the division of your assets. Remember, in most states a spouse is entitled to a share of a property's value. A court approval likely is necessary.

Don't forget. Many states may consider other factors in the settlement besides strictly assets. For example, if one spouse put the other through school, it's possible the courts could award more to that spouse.

In considering whether to award alimony, courts consider many of the same factors they consider in dividing up assets.

For tax purposes, alimony usually is treated as income to the spouse who receives it and as a deduction from the income of the person paying it.

You'll also need to iron out child support, which is a requirement for underage children. Typically, it is based on a formula set by each state that considers the parents' income and number of children. Failure to pay child support

☞ *Hot Tip* • • •

Don't depend on alimony, which is a court-ordered payment to an ex-spouse. Most alimony settlements have a time limit and end upon remarriage of the former spouse.

• • • • •

! HOW TO COMMUNICATE

• • • • •

Perhaps one of the hardest parts of getting a divorce is cushioning the blow to the people you love most—particularly your children. Even if you're on bad terms with each other, neither of you, we're sure, want the children to suffer.

Experts suggest that you:

- Have a chat with your children and explain why you're getting a divorce. Be sure they know the divorce is not their fault. Don't put down the other parent.
- Let them know if you're going to move. They need to know where you will live and where they will go to school.
- Help your children express feelings about the divorce.
- Be patient with them. Young children often feel depressed, while some have trouble sleeping. Others may wet their beds.

• • • • •

may result in garnishing of wages, intercepted tax refunds, and even jail, in some cases.

Child support is not tax deductible for the paying spouse or taxed as income for the receiver. The IRS considers payments child support if a reduction occurs around the time a child reaches 18, 21, or the state's age of majority.

You can't get out of paying alimony or child support if you declare bankruptcy, although you can attempt to have payments changed.

When Your Spouse Can't Care for Himself or Herself

OK, you've done what 50 percent of marriages haven't been able to do. You've stayed married and had a happy life together, but suddenly, one of you becomes physically or mentally difficult to deal with—we're talking really, this time. It might be that one of you is ill, or, it could simply be old age taking its toll and making everyday functions difficult to handle. Whatever the situation, you realize the time is coming where something has to be done!

Where to start?

If you perceive your spouse might soon need more care, it's best to plan as far in advance as possible. Our advice:

- Get an attorney to review and update all the paperwork we discussed with you earlier on in the book—living wills, durable power of attorney, and health care power of attorneys or agents.
- Consider how you'll pay for nursing home care your spouse might eventually need. Unfortunately, Medicare and most insurance policies only cover a certain number of days, say one to two months, in a "skilled" nursing facility. That means care after an acute illness that is administered by a registered nurse or licensed practical nurse. In other words, it does not cover care in conjunction with everyday living—such as dressing, bathing, eating, walking, or going to the bathroom. Yet, many people, when they get old, are unable to these basic functions.

Again, you'll want to talk to a lawyer who is knowledgeable about this subject, but your options for covering these other activities basically are:

- Long-term care insurance
- Paying the bills, which average upward of $30,000 annually, either yourself or via a family member
- Arranging for Medicaid to pick up the tab by transferring your assets into an irrevocable Medicaid trust or to your family

You'll also want to review your state's laws to determine exactly how much of your income, as a spouse, the nursing home may claim if your spouse outlives your assets. Of course, if you begin any transfer of assets, any gifts of at least $10,000 that you make to children, friends, or relatives are subject to a federal gift tax. Plus, your spouse may lose eligibility for Medicaid if assets were transferred within 36 months of the application or 60 months if you have assets in a living trust.

If long-term care insurance is a consideration, the National Association of Insurance Commissioners suggests looking for long-term care insurance policies with these standards:

> **☞ Hot Tip • • •**
>
> **F**or up-to-date quotes on long-term care insurance call Long Term Care Quote at 800-587-3279.
>
> • • • • •

> **☞ Hot Tip • • •**
>
> **A**s of this writing, the consensus among financial planners is that American Express Life Assurance Co., Fortis, John Hancock Mutual Life Insurance Co., CNA, and The Travelers Insurance have the best overall long-term care policies. But they also are the most expensive and may not fit everyone's needs.
>
> • • • • •

- At least one year of nursing home or health care coverage, including intermediate and custodial care. Make certain nursing home or home health care benefits are not limited to "skilled" care.
- Coverage for Alzheimer's disease, should the policyholder develop the disease after purchasing the policy.

- An inflation protection option. There should be a choice among automatically increasing the initial benefit level on an annual basis, a guaranteed right to periodically increase the benefit levels without providing evidence of insurability, and covering a specific percentage of actual and reasonable charges.
- A guarantee that the policy cannot be canceled, nonrenewed, or otherwise terminated because you get older or suffer deterioration in physical and mental health.
- The right to return a policy within 30 days after you have purchased it and receive a premium refund, if, for any reason, you don't want it.
- No requirements that policyholders must first be hospitalized in order to receive nursing home benefits or home health care benefits; must first receive skilled nursing home care before receiving intermediate or custodial nursing home care, or must first receive nursing home care before receiving benefits for home health care.

In addition, you want to:

- Only buy a policy from a financially sound insurance company. You want insurers rated at least A+ by A. M. Best, and AA in claims-paying ability from Standard & Poor's or Moody's.
- Make sure your premiums can't be raised just because you went into a nursing home.
- Compare nursing homes' daily costs.
- Consider saving about 15 percent of the cost of a policy by having a 90-day waiting period.
- Be sure to get coverage even though you have had medical problems in the past. Good policies will pay for care if you need help to perform two or three of the following Activities for Daily Living (ADLs): eating, bathing, dressing, walking, or going to the bathroom.
- Lifetime coverage costs about 50 percent more than coverage for two or three years, which is the average length of stay in a home.
- Check whether you get retroactive coverage if your insurance company comes out with an improved policy.

**Bet You
Didn't Know**

• • • • •

Don't need to go the a nursing home, but need some help? There are some options:

- Home sharing. You are matched up with other younger people who can help with services, perhaps in exchange for lower-cost housing.
- Senior housing. This is often made available at lower prices through state, federal, and local governments.
- Adult day care. If your spouse is still able to get around, he or she may benefit from adult day care, which generally costs less than a residential facility. Sometimes Medicaid even will pick up the tab.
- Continuing care retirement community. Continuing care homes facilities provide meals, activities, and 24-hour medical and personal care. There may be an upfront fee plus a monthly fee, or simply a monthly fee that can run from $1,000 and up. It may cost extra to take advantage of certain services, and the cost may increase as you require more care. For information on continuing care retirement communities, contact: The American Association of Homes for the Aging, AHA Publications, 901 E St., Suite 500, Washington, DC 20004-2037 (202-783-2242).
- Assisted living facility. This provides apartment units: group meals, and daily maid, linen, and laundry services. There also may be regular medical checkups. These facilities often provide the custodial care that is available in a nursing home. However, nursing coverage may be limited.

• • • • •

If you or your spouse must go into some kind of care facility, any institution receiving Medicare/Medicaid funding is required to abide by a Patients' Bill of Rights. Among the rights you are entitled to:

- Free choice. The right to choose a personal attending physician and be informed in advance about care and treatment.
- The right to be free from physical or mental abuse, corporal punishment, involuntary seclusion, and any physical or chemical restraints imposed for purposes of discipline or convenience.
- The right to privacy with regard to accommodations, medical treatment, written and telephone communications, visits and meetings of family or resident groups.

- Confidentiality of personal and clinical records.
- The right to receive notice before the room or roommate of the resident in the facility is changed.
- The right to voice grievances with respect to treatment or care.
- The right of the resident to organize and participate in resident groups in the facility and the right of the resident's family to meet with other residents.
- The right to participate in social, religious, and community activities that do not interfere with the rights of other residents.

☞ *Hot Tip* • • •

Whenever there is a death, financial planners advise you to take things slowly with your money. A lot of scam artists can come out of the closet. Don't make any major financial decisions. Don't take advice from people you don't know well—or even those you do if they might have a financial incentive. Never pay for anything your spouse supposedly ordered—if it's legitimate that will be discovered at probate.

• • • • •

Dealing with Death

The death of your spouse might well be the hardest thing you'll ever have to cope with. Hopefully, you've taken precautions we outlined in Chapter 11, so at least some of the financial problems that accompany this time of sorrow will be minimized.

Meanwhile, you may have the traumatic task of making funeral arrangements and providing accurate personal information about your spouse for death certificates and obituaries. Take your time deciding what to do about your property. You only want to act on your large assets when you've had time to carefully analyze the situation.

If your spouse has a small or sizable estate and/or no will at all, contact an attorney who will see the will through probate court and provide ongoing advice.

Figure 14.1

• • • • •

Dealing with Death Checklist

1. It's tough to think straight at a difficult time like this. But upon notifying friends and relatives, newspapers, alumni associations, and organizations of your loss, you'll need to start taking these steps:

Round up:

____ Ten certified copies of your spouse's death certificate, for which there may be a small charge, from the funeral director, state department of vital statistics, or county health department. You'll need these certificates for each claim of benefits you may be entitled to.

____ All insurance policies.

____ Five copies of your marriage license to claim benefits.

____ The original will, signed by the deceased and witnesses, often in a safe deposit box, or with a lawyer, and copies.

____ Copies of certificate of honorable discharge if your spouse was a veteran. If you can't find a copy, write to the Department of Defense's National Personnel Record Center, 9700 Page Boulevard, St. Louis, MO 63132 or phone: 314-538-4261 for the Army; 314-538-4141 for the Navy, Marines, or Coast Guard, or 314-538-4243 for the Air Force.

____ Your spouse's Social Security number, which should be on past tax returns.

____ Most recent tax return.

____ Name of his or her financial adviser(s).

____ Children's birth certificates.

____ Naturalization papers (if applicable).

2. Contact an attorney and, unless trust arrangements were made, file for probate, which is the legal process of proving the will's validity.

3. Contact an accountant.

4. Apply for any benefits you may be entitled to:

____ Life insurance, including policies through organizations and credit life or mortgage payment insurance

____ Veteran's benefits

____ Retirement plan

____ Social Security

____ Employee benefits

Figure 14.1

. . . . .

Dealing with Death Checklist (cont.)

5. Change titles.
___ House
___ Bank accounts
___ Credit cards
___ Car
___ Stocks, bonds, mutual funds, other investments
___ Safe deposit box

6. Change beneficiaries.
___ Your own will
___ Your own life insurance policies
___ Your own retirement accounts

7. File and pay taxes.

In most cases, joint bank and security accounts automatically will revert to you. Any accounts in your spouse's name exclusively will have to go through probate.

But until the will has gone through probate, only the will, life insurance policies, or documents relating to death generally may be removed from a safe deposit box.

There are numerous other things that have to be taken care of such as:

☞ Hot Tip . . .

Although a funeral home typically will prepare a basic obituary for local newspapers, you might wish to supply additional information.

• • • • •

- Claim life insurance, pension, health and veteran's benefits.
- Claim union or professional association benefits.
- You'll need to change titles to any property you owned together, such as the house, car, and investments.

- Change credit cards and pay off any of the deceased's outstanding balances. Notify other lenders.
- Prepare spouse's tax return and or federal estate tax returns.

If your spouse has contributed to Social Security for a long time, you may be entitled to survivor benefits. However, you must file a claim to collect.

Go to your nearest Social Security office, and meet with a representative. Retain the name and phone number of the person you meet with in case you

Bet You Didn't Know

• • • •

Veterans are entitled to free burial in a national cemetery. Grave markers are free. There also may be educational assistance and medical care for dependents. Contact your local office of the Department of Veterans Affairs for instructions and forms.

• • • • •

need more information. You'll need to bring the death certificate, marriage certificate, Social Security numbers, and W-2 forms of your spouse.

At death, Social Security typically pays a special one-time payment of $255 if your spouse had enough work credits. You may be eligible for survivor benefits if you're age 60, or 50 if you're disabled. There may be additional benefits for unmarried children under age 18 or up to age 19 if they're still attending elementary or secondary school. Plus, a widow or widower can get benefits at any age if he or she has a child under 16 or a disabled child.

Apart from the emotional loss, you're now in an entirely new boat financially. You may have financial responsibilities you didn't have before. Possibly your spouse handled all the investing, and you're not even sure what you have. Hopefully, you've already read our earlier chapters and that's not the case. But nevertheless, you'll have to try to figure out exactly where you sit.

If your spouse worked, you may have to exist without that added income. Or, you might find yourself left with added income that you suddenly will have to invest on your own.

You'll want to go back to Chapters 9 and 11 and redo some of the budgeting and estate planning exercises we suggested earlier—but this time, based on your new financial situation.

Gearing Up for Those Early Bird Specials

Now you can relax. No more hassles of getting up at 6 AM and sending kids to school or fighting rush hour traffic. Your time is your own. You can do what you want. Play your cards right and you can use your free time to travel, play golf, go to ball games, hit the flea markets or shows, or shop. Unfortunately, although you may have all the time in the world, you still have bills to pay. So you need to make certain your money will last. More people are living into their 90s. Couples in their 60s may have a good 25 years or more ahead of them. In addition to coughing up enough money to survive, you'll need to agree on how and where you will spend your golden years together. This chapter is designed to inspire an emotionally happy and healthy retirement, and financially, at least, to continue a relationship that's nothing but first-class.

How to Enjoy Your Retirement While Living on a Fixed Income

Fortunately, when you retire to Florida, Arizona, Texas, or some other senior citizen southern hot spot like North Carolina, you'll learn about one of the best deals on the face of the earth—"early bird specials."

You can get full-course meals from terrific restaurants—often for little as half price—provided that you eat by 5:30 or 6 PM. Live in another area? These deals often go by other names, like "pre-theater specials" or "sunset dinners." In fact, we try to take advantage of all these types of offers wherever we go. Two steak dinners, with vegetables, salad, and coffee cost us $18. We can have Thai or Chinese for less.

The early bird specials are just one of the little perks you finally get to take advantage of when you start hitting your senior years. Chances are, you'll also start qualifying for bus transportation discounts in your area. Airlines frequently offer fare discounts. Take United Airlines' Silver Wings Plus Travel Program and Continental's Freedom Passport. You get discounts on air, hotel, and rental cars. You'll pay some up-front charges for these services, but it's worth it if you plan to travel.

Like to take a train? If you're at least 62, you get a 15 percent discount on Amtrak. For $199, less 15 percent, you get Amtrak's "All Aboard Fares." You can travel to five places in either the Western, Central, or Eastern regions of the United States. Go to all three regions for $339 less 15 percent.

You've certainly worked hard enough to earn your leisure time, so you want to take full advantage of it. That means spending as little as possible so that you can have the most fun for your buck.

☞ Hot Tip • • •

Get a free copy of AARP's 99 Travel Tips for Mature Travelers by calling 800-784-0935.

• • • • •

If possible, you might want to refer to some of the cost saving measures we listed in Chapter 1.

Consider organizations that provide travel and entertainment discounts. The American Association of Retired Persons (AARP), for example, offers discounts on travel, consumer goods, medicine, and health and life insurance. Plus, you get a monthly magazine and newsletter that will keep you informed on important issues affecting seniors. It costs just $8 per year to belong to AARP.

Call AARP at 202-434-2277 for membership information. Then call 800-322-2282 ext. 6589 and ask for the AARP Investment Program Information. You'll be well on your way to successfully managing your retirement dollars.

> ## Bet You
> ## Didn't Know
>
> • • • • •
>
> **E**njoy these retirement perks together:
>
> 1. Over 55 and interested in living on a college campus for a week? Elder Hostel provides week-long residential learning programs hosted by some 2,300 institutions in the United States and overseas, ranging from colleges to theaters, art schools, and museums. Average cost is $350 including lodging, meals, daily classes, and extracurricular activities. For information, contact: Elder Hostel, 75 Federal St., Boston, MA 02110-1941 (617-426-7788).
>
> 2. The following travel agencies specialize in senior travel packages: ElderTreks, 597 Markham St., Toronto, Ontario M6G2L7, (800-741-7956), features more exotic trips for persons over 50. Saga International Holidays Ltd., 222 Berkeley St., Boston, MA 02116 (800-343-0273).
>
> 3. You might enjoy renting or buying into a senior development. A number of condo complexes, particularly in some of the resort areas, offer bus service, pools, tennis courts, and golf courses. They have restaurants and clubhouses with low-cost professional entertainment.
>
> Check with your local universities. Often seniors are permitted to audit classes for free.
>
> • • • • •

The American Automobile Association provides emergency road service, as well as travel benefits. So do many auto clubs.

Also, check with your local Chamber of Commerce for businesses that offer deals to seniors. Merchants don't always advertise the benefits they provide for seniors, so don't be afraid to ask wherever you go. In most areas, you can save as much as 75 percent off the cost of movie tickets. There also are a lot of free concerts and activities especially for seniors. Plus, seniors get to pay less at places like Disney World, museums, and zoos.

Have fun!

As usual, that M-word is the catalyst that gives you power to do many of the things you'd like to do—even in your senior years. So just as when you were younger, you want to take steps to ensure you won't run out. Plus, you

! How to Communicate

· · · · ·

Thinking about retirement? To ensure a content and harmonious life together, we suggest you grab a pencil and paper and take the following steps:

1. Agree to draw up a contract detailing how you each would like to spend your senior years. Of course, this contract may be subject to change. But at least it sets the tone of your decision-making together.

2. Establish, if you haven't already, which of you will work, and until what age each of you intends to work. Will the work be part time or full time?

3. Agree on where you'd both like to live. First focus on the geographic location. Can't reach an agreement? You can always be a snowbird. Spend your summers in one area and winters in another. Then discuss the type of home you'd like to have. Do you still need that three-bedroom, two-bath home, or might you prefer to downsize to a condo?

4. Figure out, based on the financial analysis we'll help you through later in this chapter, how much each of you can afford to spend each week and still live comfortably. Agree to stick to that plan.

5. Agree on an investment strategy to help you both get the most out of your retirement kitty. You might want to seek the help of a financial planner to get you started on the right foot.

6. Agree on the best way—for both tax and estate planning and estate planning wise—to withdraw money from your pension and retirement plans. You may need help from an accountant or attorney on this one.

7. Take care of all your medical, dental, and optional needs while you're still working and have good insurance coverage.

· · · · ·

want to amass enough dough to do all the things you've ever wanted to do in the time you have left. All of this calls for, you guessed it, more planning.

There's yet another reason to brainstorm together and organize your retirement. Research studying the major landmarks of life, including retirement, indicates that planning and knowing what to expect makes for a more positive experience than unexpected crises or unrealized goals. That's why you need to sit down together right in the beginning—before you retire, if possible—to discuss some of the important retirement issues to come.

Social Security, Your Pension, and Savings

As we promised you earlier in this book, you probably won't be spending money commuting to work or on entertainment, clothes, and taxes like you used to. Hopefully, you've paid off the mortgage, or you'll pay it off shortly, and chances are you've paid up on your life insurance. That's a nice bundle of cash you needn't shell out any more, thank goodness.

Unfortunately, though, you'll need to consider that medical expenses may take a growing chunk of your budget. After you hit age 65, Medicare takes care of many of the bills. Medicare part A covers part of your hospital bills, some nursing home or home health care coverage, and hospice care. Part B covers inpatient and outpatient doctor services, outpatient hospital services, and some medical equipment and supplies. But you'll need insurance to cover the gap. So shop around for coverage.

You'll be spending more on leisure activities. Plus the cost of fuel, food, and clothing probably has risen, and will continue to rise, due to inflation, we're sorry to report.

Many experts predict that as the population ages and Social Security benefits decline, more seniors will opt to work part time to help make ends meet. In fact, a 1997 USA Today/CNN/Gallup poll of 77 million Americans born between 1946 and 1964 indicated three-quarters actually would choose to continue working. It certainly feels better to have a little extra cash on hand. Besides it's healthy to keep busy.

Assuming you do want to hang up your spikes, overall the Social Security Administration estimates, Social Security would cover about 25 percent if you averaged $60,000 annually during your working years. Another 20 percent will come from your pension and a whopping 30 percent either from working after you retire or other sources of investment income. Keep in mind that the more money you make, the lower the proportion that Social Security income will replace.

Today you can collect 80 percent of your Social Security when you are 62 years old. Wait until age 65, and you will collect the full amount. Those born after 1943, however, won't be able to take full Social Security pay until they hit age 66. And those born after 1960 won't tap their full benefits until age 67.

Provided that you've socked away money in your company pension plan, a variable annuity or IRA, and other investments, as we've suggested earlier, you should have the resources you need to live on.

Well, we've given you the scoop on Social Security (see Chapters 4 and 10). Now total up how much you'll be able to collect from your other retirement savings accounts including IRAs, company pensions, annuities, and life insurance, plus, any other investment income (see Figure 15.1).

Figure 15.1 • • • • •

Annual Income from Retirement Assets

IRA or pension	$_____
Annuity	_____
Other savings	_____
Real estate	_____
Life insurance cash value	_____
Trust assets	_____
Social Security	_____
TOTAL	$_____

Once you see how much you've stashed away, look at what you may be spending during retirement for rent or mortgage, clothes, food, health care, debt payments, utilities, insurance premiums, entertainment, transportation, travel, taxes, and miscellaneous (see Figure 15.2).

Your housing costs, including insurance, utilities, taxes, and rent or mortgage, should be 30 percent of your income or less. Figure the cost of just about everything will rise about $3\frac{1}{2}$ percent per year. So each year, multiply your annual expenses by 1.35 to give you an estimate of how much more things will cost you.

Once you've analyzed this picture, you can figure out what you need to do to save. Buying a good used car may save you some money.

You can save 70 percent on prescriptions by buying generic drugs rather than brand-name ones.

Figure 15.2

• • • • •

Expenses During Retirement as a Percent of Your Income

Food: 15% $_____

Housing: 30%   _____

Transportation: 10%   _____

Insurance: Varies   _____

Entertainment: Varies   _____

Health Care: Varies but may make up a large part of your expenses   _____

Taxes: Varies   _____

Debts: Varies   _____

TOTAL $_____

As you consider ways to cut your costs so that you can enjoy your life more, consider how you can increase your investments as well. As we indicated earlier, senior citizens are living much longer today than they used to and need their money to hold out. Remember, it's important for your investments to keep pace with inflation.

You can get some of the growth you need from mutual funds that invest in common stocks. You get the income from bonds, bond funds, annuities, utility stocks, or municipal bond funds.

As we indicated earlier in this book, historically stocks have grown at about 7 percent more than the inflation rate over the years.

Bonds historically have grown at about a 5 percent annual rate. T-bills, money funds, and short-term bank CDs have grown at about 3 percent.

☞ *Hot Tip* • • •

It's always a good idea to keep some of your investments in at least a good growth and income fund. Funds we like that carry top ratings from Morningstar Inc., Chicago, and Value Line, New York, include:

- Vanguard S&P 500 Fund, which invests in the 500 largest companies traded on the New York Stock Exchange.
- AARP Growth and Income Fund, which invests in large company stocks that pay high dividend yields.
- Scudder Growth and Income, which also invests in high-yielding, dividend-paying stocks.
- T. Rowe Price Equity Income Fund, which also invests in stocks that pay high dividends.
- Lexington Corporate Leaders, which has owned the same 30 blue chip stocks for more than five decades.
- Invesco Industrial Income, which also invests in rock solid companies.
- Safeco Equity, which has been one of the best performing stock funds over the past 50 years.
- Neuberger & Berman Guardian Fund, buys undervalued large company stocks.
- Investment Company of America has one of the best track records over the past five decades.
- Putnam Growth & Income is another fund with a solid track record.

• • • • •

The rule of thumb is the longer you have to invest, the more you should have in stocks or stock funds. So if you are in your 60s, you need the growth to help your assets keep pace with inflation.

But once you get well into your 80s and 90s, you need to concentrate on keeping what you have. So you should have less invested in stocks and more in less risky income-producing investments like CDs, Treasury bonds, and utility stocks or annuities. If your need for income is low and you have ten years to invest, you should keep at least 70 percent in a well-managed stock fund, 20 percent invested for income in a bond fund, and 10 percent in a money fund.

What if you need your principal over the next three years? You should have 50 percent in a money fund, 50 percent in a bond fund, and zero in stock funds.

Taking Your Retirement Pay

Once you reach your retirement years, you finally get to take out all the money you worked so hard to save. Of course, Uncle Sam sure doesn't make this very easy. Your objective, assuming you can ever figure out the IRS's strict and convoluted rules, generally is to withdraw as little as possible so that more of your nest egg grows tax-deferred for as long as possible.

Unfortunately, the IRS requires you to begin withdrawing money from your IRA or 401(k) by April 1 of the year after you hit age 70$\frac{1}{2}$—not age 70, mind you! If your withdrawals or "distributions" are less than IRS rules permit, Uncle Sam hits you with a 50 percent excise tax on the shortfall.

There are a number of ways to handle these wrinkles. Naming the right beneficiary is the first step. Financial planners warn you not to name your estate, a trust, or charity as the sole IRA beneficiary. The reason is that if you die before the date you're required to start withdrawing your stash, all the IRA money must be paid out in one shot. That means, based on the wisdom of the IRS, that all of the income tax is due by the end of the fifth calendar year following the year you die.

There are two basic ways to take your IRA pay. But these methods also apply to your 401(k) company pension plan or other profit sharing plans where you make tax-deductible contributions:

- Fixed payment method. All the money must be withdrawn out of your IRA or retirement plan based on your life expectancy. For example, someone age 71 has a life expectancy of 15 years, according to—you guessed it—IRS life expectancy tables. So in year one, one-fifteenth of your money is withdrawn. Assuming you have $100,000 in your retirement kitty, you'd have to withdraw $6,536. Ten years later, you would take $18,868 out of your IRA. By the time you hit age 86, you would have deleted most of your account.

- Recalculation method. With this technique, you get an extra few years for your money to grow tax-deferred. That's because every year you get to recalculate your life expectancy based upon the IRS tables. This means less is taken out of your kitty because each year you live, the IRS figures you'll be around an extra few more years. The same 71 year old would withdraw $6,536 from his or her IRA in the first year. But in year ten, the amount is $11,236. By the time the 71 year old reaches age 86, there still would be a few years of tax-deferred IRA income left to rely on.

Say you name a spouse as beneficiary. Another strange IRS rule kicks in. If you die before you are required to take distribution, your spouse has the option to wait until the date you would have reached 70½ to do it. This way, the payments can be stretched out over your surviving spouse's life expectancy.

A better option if one spouse is significantly younger than the other, say some financial planners, might be for the surviving wife or husband instead to treat the IRA as his or her own. This

Bet You Didn't Know

• • • • •

Made it together to your retirement years? Despite what the tabloids say, you're in some star-studded company. As of this writing:

- Paul Newman and Joanne Woodward. Married 31 years.
- Steve Lawrence and Eydie Gorme. Married 43 years.
- Jerry Stiller and Anne Meara. Married 43 years.

• • • • •

way, he or she gets to defer taking distributions until age 70½. For example, if Jack dies at age 69, his 62-year-old wife, Mary, can claim the IRA as her own and avoid taking distributions for more than eight years—until age 70½. This way, she also gets to name another person as a beneficiary to the IRA.

Most people leave their retirement savings to their spouses. Widows or widowers typically leave the money to their children or grandchildren. If you are married or have a younger beneficiary, the IRS lets you base payouts on a joint life expectancy using the younger person. Then, you can recalculate the joint life expectancy each year.

Because one person is younger, the joint life expectancy is greater. So you get to take less money out of the IRA. Unfortunately, the IRS limits that age difference to ten years. So if you happen to be 70¾ years old, forget the idea of naming your one-year-old grandchild as joint beneficiary. He or she would have to be 60¾ under IRS payout rules.

Phyllis Bonfield of the American Society of CLU and ChFC, Bryn Mawr, Pennsylvania, points out yet another major downside to using a young beneficiary. "Recalculating your life expectancy can carry a stiff penalty when the beneficiary isn't your spouse," she says. "A beneficiary who is not a spouse would be required to greatly increase the amount withdrawn from the IRA under IRS rules."

Making the Most of Your Pension

Once you are about to collect your company pension, make certain you check the right payout option. Of

Bet You Didn't Know

• • • • •

It's not just income tax from Uncle Sam you have to worry about with your retirement savings. There also are estate and other tax issues to contend with. Retirement money can go to your spouse's estate tax free.

But if your estate is larger than $625,000 when you die, taxes can hit with a vengeance—particularly if your retirement savings have never been taxed before your heirs get it! Fortunately, Uncle Sam is phasing in a higher estate tax threshold, which is slated to reach $1 million in 2006.

In fact, in a substantial estate that includes a retirement plan, there may be federal and state income taxes, excise tax, federal estate tax, and sometimes state estate taxes. Combined, these taxes can eat up as much as a whopping 65 to 90 percent of an estate!

• • • • •

course, you want both you and your spouse to get the most income possible out of it.

The federal Employee Retirement Income Security Act provides two options to most married employees when one is entitled to a pension from his or her employer. Option A provides a lifetime pension for the retired employee, but if the employee dies before his or her spouse, the spouse gets nothing. This is known as the maximum pension or "life only" payout option.

By contrast, Option B, known as "the joint and survivor option," provides a lifetime pension reduced by about 20 percent for the retired employee. If the employee dies first, 50 to 75 percent of the monthly income is continued to the surviving spouse. Most married couples opt for the joint and survivor option.

> ### ☞ Hot Tip • • •
>
> If you selected the joint and survivor payout on a pension and the retiree outlives the spouse, you could lose benefits.
>
> So, if there is any doubt about the health of your spouse, financial planners advise taking a lump-sum payment from the pension plan and transferring it into an IRA. This way, money must be paid out over the joint life expectancy of the couple when you reach age $70\frac{1}{2}$, resulting in higher payouts compared with payments from the pension plan or insurance annuity. Plus, unlike with a pension plan, the IRA money goes to beneficiaries when the second spouse dies.
>
> • • • • •

Financial planners, though, say it could pay to investigate alternatives, so that you don't necessarily give yourself a paycut in return for your spouse's continued income.

One option to consider while you're still in your 50s is to choose the maximum pension payout and purchase a cash value life insurance policy to provide death benefits to the surviving spouse. The proceeds from the policy would pay as much as or more than the surviving spouse would receive from the joint pension payout. Yet, the retired employee winds up with a larger monthly check.

This idea can work if the pension has a low payout and insurance can be purchased at a reasonable cost.

Other Sources of Retirement Income: Immediate Annuity and Reverse Annuity Mortgage

Now that you've got a fix on your Social Security, IRAs, and pension, there are other sources of retirement income you can turn to, if necessary.

With an immediate annuity, you invest a lump sum of money and the insurance company agrees to pay you income for as long as you live. Immediate annuities may pay a fixed amount of income, set by the insurance company, based on its investments. Or, they can pay a variable amount, based on the performance of mutual funds you select. As of this writing, most annuities, on a $100,000 investment, were paying about $800 to $1,000 a month for as long as you live.

The big advantage of an immediate annuity is that regardless of what type of immediate annuity you choose, you know it will pay you a monthly check for as long as you live. If you live to be 200 years old, you'll still collect.

You even can adjust the size of your immediate annuity payments based on the type of contract you choose.

With one of the most common immediate annuity contracts, "ten year certain and life," you get your income for life. But if you die before the ten-year period expires, the checks automatically go to a designated beneficiary for the rest of the ten years.

There is one other major benefit to immediate annuities. You only pay taxes on that part of the income that represents earnings.

Of course, as with any other investments that sound too good to be true, immediate annuities have their drawbacks:

- The greatest problem is that while this insurance instrument promises you income for life, unfortunately (or fortunately), you don't know when you're going to die. If you die before

> ### ☞ Hot Tip • • •
>
> **W**ant larger monthly payouts? Select a "life only" immediate annuity. This way, you can take larger payments based on your life expectancy. Unfortunately, you'll pay for this advantage. With this type of contract, the insurance company pockets anything left of your investment when you die, so your heirs lose out.
>
> • • • • •

you get back all your principal and earnings in the form of periodic payments, the insurance company pockets the balance of your investment. That is, unless you select a period certain policy that allows you to designate a beneficiary. Even then, the period for which that beneficiary can collect is limited.

- You can't get out of an immediate annuity contract. Once you make your investment, you're stuck. You can't change the terms either.
- With a fixed immediate annuity, your payments are fixed based on your life expectancy. As inflation increases over the years, the purchasing power of your annuity payments shrinks. You may or may not have this problem, however, with a variable immediate annuity, because payments are based on the performance of the mutual funds you choose. Typically, variable immediate annuities have a rate floor of 3 to 5 percent.
- You have no federal guarantees with an immediate annuity. If you pick an insurance company that is financially weak today, it could be gone tomorrow. If you consider an immediate annuity, stick only with the safest insurance companies rated at least A+ by A.M. Best or B+ by Weiss Research, and AA claims-paying rating by Standard & Poor's or Moody's.

Reverse Mortgage

With a reverse mortgage, by contrast, you're actually taking out a loan against the equity in your home and receiving payments—generally until you move, sell the home, or die.

This type of loan is expected to become more widely available in the future through financial institutions.

Often, with a reverse mortgage, you pay either an insurance fee or higher rate so that you needn't worry about paying back the loan when you die. Generally, the older you are and the more equity you have in your home, the more you can borrow. Like any other loan, there are rates and fees you need to compare before signing on the dotted line.

A reverse mortgage can be in the form of a lump-sum loan or it can be a credit line from which you borrow when you need it. Or you can simply obtain monthly advances until you die or move from the home. Then the loan is repaid after your house is sold, or the balance comes out of your estate. Some lenders may also take a cut of your home's appreciation.

> ☞ **Hot Tip** • • •
>
> For more information, and an updated list of lenders offering reverse mortgages, send $1 and a self-addressed, stamped envelope to Reverse Mortgage Locator, Suite 115, 7373 147th St., Apple Valley, MN 55124.
>
> • • • • •

Best Places to Retire Together

Do you both really want to stay in the same home you've lived in since you've been married? If your children are gone, perhaps you can sell your home at a profit and use the extra cash you've received to enjoy your retirement.

Or maybe you would prefer a warmer climate. Or a colder climate for that matter. Do you prefer the city or suburbs? Consider what you like to do—golf, swim, dine out, hike, participate in planned activities, or go to the theater or movies. After all, you have the rest of your lives to enjoy together.

We suggest that before you decide where you'd like to enjoy your final years—assuming you may want to change your abode—first consider what characteristics are important to you. Do you want to avoid high-crime areas? If so, you may want to stay clear of places like New Orleans and Washington, D.C.

Is money an issue? In that case, downsizing might sound like an attractive option. Plus, you'll probably want to consider an area that has a low cost of living and low taxes. You've heard of Kokomo Islands, immortalized in the Beach Boys' hit, "Key Largo?" Well, unfortunately, no such place exists. However, if you move to the small town of Kokomo in Indiana, you'll be hitting the nation's most affordable housing market, based on the National Association of Home Builders' Housing Opportunity Index. You'll also have more disposable income if you live in low-cost places like Brownsville, Texas; Mount Dora, Florida; or Asheville, North Carolina. By contrast, it can cost you twice as much if you happen to like Manhattan and all that goes with it.

You'll also want to keep an eye on taxes. There is no state income tax in Florida, Alaska, Nevada, South Dakota, Texas, Washington, or Wyoming, reports the National Conference of State Legislatures in Denver. Tennessee and New Hampshire only tax income and dividends. Meanwhile some 26 states exempt Social Security from taxes. Hawaii, Illinois, Pennsylvania, and Mississippi add full pensions to the list of state income tax exemptions. By contrast if you live in Virginia, the state will clip you for about 8 percent of your income. Even if there's no state income tax, consider property taxes—they too can take their bite. The less you pay in taxes the more you can put in your own pocket.

Perhaps one of you needs medical care. You may want to consider being near some of the top doctors. In that case, New York, Boston, Los Angeles, and Philadelphia have some of the nation's top-shelf medical teaching hospitals. Oops. Maybe Washington, D.C. also comes back into the picture! Also, Rochester, Minnesota is home of the Mayo Clinic.

Living year around down South is a lot less expensive. Taxes and the cost of living are typically lower. Plus, you generally need just one set of clothes you can wear year around. But you have to put up with hot muggy summers and lots of storms. Live on the coast line and you'd better be prepared for hurricane season from June through November in places like Florida, Louisiana, Alabama, and the Southeast coastline. Live in Southern California and you have to deal with earthquakes. Live in the Southwest and you must cope with water shortages, sand storms, and temperatures over 100 degrees. In Oregon and Washington, there's lots and lots of rain. If you're considering a dream spot near the ocean, don't forget to add the cost of flood insurance to your budget.

Consider family and friends. You might need them more as it becomes more difficult to do things on your own. Perhaps, you'd like to stay close to them. You typically can gather information on any locations you're interested in, by writing the local Chambers of Commerce.

Use the handy check list in Figure 15.3 to help you make this important decision.

There are several sources for information about where to retire. Kenneth Stern of Rancho Bernardo, California, has written an excellent book, *50 Fabulous Places To Retire In America*, published by Career Press. That's a good place to start.

Figure 15.3

• • • • •
Places to Retire Checklist

To help sort out your ideal retirement location, list areas you are considering in the Retirement Location columns below. Then research answers to the information in each category, and write, if not hard figures, at least a numerical rank among your listed locations in the appropriate box. Once you have researched this information together, you will be equipped to discuss intelligently which retirement location each of you would prefer.

Category	Retirement Location 1	Retirement Location 2	Retirement Location 3	Retirement Location 4	Retirement Location 5
Cost of Living					
Taxes:					
State	_____	_____	_____	_____	_____
Property	_____	_____	_____	_____	_____
Estate	_____	_____	_____	_____	_____
Climate:					
Temperature	_____	_____	_____	_____	_____
Storm activity	_____	_____	_____	_____	_____
Leisure Activities:					
Sports	_____	_____	_____	_____	_____
Discussion groups	_____	_____	_____	_____	_____
Theater	_____	_____	_____	_____	_____
Restaurants	_____	_____	_____	_____	_____
Education	_____	_____	_____	_____	_____
Job opportunities	_____	_____	_____	_____	_____
Health care	_____	_____	_____	_____	_____
Crime	_____	_____	_____	_____	_____

Money magazine publishes a "best places to retire" list. Each month, the magazine's *Retire With Money* newsletter lists attractive places to retire. Also check your local bookstore for other publications.

Whatever location you select for your golden years, we're sure you'll continue to be happy—particularly if you both take the time to plan your retirement together.

Getting Info on the Financial Strength of Insurance Companies

A. M. Best
800-424-2378
http://www.ambest.com/

Standard & Poors
212-208-1527
http://www.insure.com/ratings/tabFrame.html

Moody's Investor Services
212-553-0377
http://www.moodys.com/economic/ecoindex.htm

Duff & Phelps
312-368-3157
http://www.dcrco.com/PRODUCTS/P_INS.HTM

Weiss Research
800-289-9222

Financial Planners

National Association of Personal Financial Advisers
800-366-2732
http://www.napfa.org/

Institute for Certified Financial Planners
800-282-7526
http://www.icfp.org/

International Association for Financial Planning
404-845-0111
http://www.iafp.org/

Licensed Independent Network of CPA Financial Planners
800-737-2727
http://www.lincpfp.com/

Check Your Credit Reports

Equifax
800-685-1111
http://www.equifax.com/

TransUnion
312-408-1400
http://transunion-dateq.com/

Experian
800-392-1122
http://www.experian.com/

Guide to Investment Regulatory Agencies

State Securities Agencies

Alabama Securities Commission
334-242-2984
http://www.scor-net.com/parstate/al.htm

Alaska Department of Commerce & Economic Development
Division of Banking, Securities & Corporations
907-465-4242
http://www.state.ak.us/local/akpages/commerce/dced.htm

Arizona Corporation Commission
Securities Division
602-542-4242
http://www.netdrct.com/test/azcorp/securities/index2.htm

California Department of Corporations
213-736-2495
http://www.corp.ca.gov/

Colorado Division of Securities
303-894-2320
http://www.state.co.us/gov-dir/regulatory-dir/sec.htm

Connecticut Department of Banking
203-240-8230
800-831-7225
http://www.state.ct.us/dob/

Delaware Department of Justice
Division of Securities
302-577-2515

District of Columbia Services Commission
Securities Division
202-626-5105

Florida Office of the Comptroller
Division of Securities
904-488-9805
800-848-3792
http://www:dbf.state.fl.us/hotlines.htm/

Georgia Office of the Secretary of State
Securities Division
Information: 404-656-2695
Complaints: 404-656-3920
http://www.sos.state.ga.us/securities/default.htm

Hawaii Department of Commerce & Consumer Affairs
Securities Commission
808-589-2730
http://www.capital-network.com/states/hi.htm

Idaho Department of Finance
Securities Bureau
208-334-3684
http://www.state.id.us/Finance/dof.htm

Illinois Office of the Secretary of State
Securities Department
217-782-2256
800-628-7937
http://www.capital-network.com/states/il.htm

Indiana Office of the Secretary of State
Securities Division
317-232-6681
800-223-8791

Iowa Department of Commerce
Insurance Division
Iowa Securities Bureau
515-281-4441
http://www.state.ia.us/government/com/ins/ins.htm

Kansas Securities Commission
913-296-3307
http://www.capital-network.com/states/ks.htm

Kentucky Department of Financial Institutions
Division of Securities
502-573-3390
http://www.dfi.state.ky.us/security/security.html

Requests for information must be in writing:
Department of Financial Institutions
477 Versailles Road
Frankton, KY 40401
Attn: David Ashley

Louisiana Securities Commission
504-568-5515
http://www.capital-network.com/states/la.htm

Requests for information must be in writing:
Louisiana Securities Commission
Energy Centre
1100 Pydras St., Suite 2250
New Orleans, LA 70163
http://www.scor-net.com/parstate/la.htm

Maine Department of Professional & Financial Regulation
Bureau of Banking, Securities Division
207-582-8760
http://www.state.me.us/pfr/sec/links.htm

Maryland Attorney General's Office
Division of Securities
410-576-6360
http://www.capital-network.com/states/md.htm

Massachusetts Secretary of the Commonwealth
Securities Division
617-727-3548
http://www.magnet.state.ma.us/sec/sct/sctidx.htm

Michigan Department of Commerce
Corporation and Securities Bureau
517-334-6200
http://www.commerce.state.mi.us/corp/

Minnesota Department of Commerce
Information: 612-296-2283
Complaints: 612-296-2488
http://www.commerce.state.mn.us/

Mississippi Office of the Secretary of State
Securities Division
601-359-6364
800-804-6364

Missouri Office of the Secretary of State
Securities Division
314-751-4136
800-721-7996
http://www.mosl.sos.state.mo.us/sos-sec/sossec.html

Montana Office of the State Auditor
Securities Department
406-444-2040
800-332-6148
http://www.sec.gov/rules/proposed/s73196/okeefel.txt

Nebraska Department of Banking & Finance
Bureau of Securities
402-471-3445
http://www.nbdf.orgl

Nevada Office of the Secretary of State
Securities Division
702-486-2440
800-758-6440
http://www.capital-network.com/states/nv.htm

New Hampshire Bureau of Securities Regulation
603-271-1463
800-994-4200
http://www.capital-network.com/states/nh.htm

New Jersey Department of Law and Public Safety
Bureau of Securities
201-504-3600
http://www.state.nj.us/lps/ca/bos.htm

New Mexico Regulation & Licensing Department
Securities Division
505-827-7140
800-704-5533
http://gsd.state.nm.us/rld/_mstr.html

New York Department of Law
Bureau of Investor Protection and Securities
212-416-8200
http://www.capital-network.com/not.htm

Requests for information must be in writing:
Attn: Alice McInerney
New York State Department of Law
Bureau of Investor Protection and Securities
120 Broadway, 23rd Floor
New York, NY 10271

North Carolina Office of the Secretary of State
Securities Division
919-733-3924
Complaints: 800-668-4507
http://www.capital-network.com/states/nc.htm

North Dakota Office of the Securities Commissioner
701-328-2910
800-297-5124
http://www.capital-network.com/states/nd.htm

Ohio Division of Securities
614-644-7381
http://www.capital-network.com/states/oh.htm

Oklahoma Department of Securities
405-235-0230
http://www.oklaosf.state.ok.us/~osc/

Oregon Department of Consumer & Business Services
Division of Finance & Corporate Securities
503-378-4387
http://www.state.or.us/agencies/44000/00040/

Pennsylvania Securities Commission
717-787-8061
800-600-0077
http://www.state.pa.us/pa_exec/securities/

Rhode Island Department of Business Regulation
Securities Division
401-277-3048
http://www.capital-network.com/states/ri.htm

South Carolina Securities Division
803-734-1087
http://www.capital-network.com/states/sc.htm

South Dakota Division of Securities
605-773-4823
http://www.capital-network.com/states/sd.htm

Tennessee Department of Commerce & Insurance
Securities Division
Information: 615-741-3187
Complaints: 615-741-5900
http://www.state.tn.us/commerce/securdiv.html

Texas State Securities Board
512-305-8332
http://www.ssb.state.tx.us/

Utah Department of Commerce
Division of Securities
801-530-6600
800-721-3233
http://www.commerce.state.ut.us/web/commerce/securit/sec.htm

Vermont Department of Banking, Insurance & Securities
Securities Division
802-828-3420
http://www.state.vt.us/dca/captive/is/isl.htm

Virginia State Corporation Commission
Division of Securities & Retail Franchising
804-371-9051
http://www.capital-network.com/states/va.htm

Washington Department of Financial Institutions
Securities Division
360-902-8760
http://www.capital-network.com/states/wa.htm

West Virginia's State Auditor's Office
Securities Division
304-558-2257
http://www.capital-network.com/states/wv.htm

Wisconsin Office of the Commissioner of Securities
608-266-3431
800-472-4325
http://www.capital-network.com/states/wi.htm

Wyoming Secretary of State
Securities Division
State Capitol Bldg.
Cheyenne, Wyoming 82002
307-777-7370
http://soswy.state.wy.us/securiti/reg_bd.htm

National Regulators

Commodity Futures Trading Commission
202-254-3067 (enforcement division)
http://www.cftc.gov/

National Association of Securities Dealers
202-728-8000 (main)
800-289-9999 (information about brokers and firms)
http://www.nasd.com/

National Futures Association
Disciplinary Information Access Line (DIAL)
200 W. Madison St., Suite 1600
Chicago Illinois 60505
800-621-3570 (national)
800-572-9400 (in Illinois)
http://www.nfa.lutures.org/menu.html

U.S. Securities and Exchange Commission
202-942-7040 (main)
1-800-SEC-0330 (complaints/consumer information)
http://www.cftech.com/brainbank/finance/secexchgcomm.html

Helpful Newsletters

Income and Safety
800-327-6720

Morningstar Mutual Funds
800-735-0700

Moneysworth
800-816-4744

Mutual Fund Forecaster
800-327-6720

The Mutual Fund Letter
800-326-6941

The NoLoad Fund X
415-986-7979

Mutual Fund Monthly
888-786-5737

Personal Finance
800-832-2330

No-Load Fund Analyst
415-989-8513

Jay Schabacker's Mutual Fund Letter
800-777-5005

The No-Load Fund Investor
914-693-7420

Value Line Mutual Fund Survey
800-284-7607

Books to Help You Manage the Family Money

The American Bar Association Guide To Family Law (New York: Times Books, 1996).

The Complete Idiot's Guide to Making Money on Wall Street, Christy Heady (New York: Alpha Books, 1996).

The Complete Idiot's Guide To Making Money With Mutual Funds, Alan Lavine and Gail Liberman (New York: Alpha Books, 1996).

The Complete Idiot's Guide to Managing Your Money, Robert K. Heady and Christy Heady (New York: Alpha Books, 1995).

Everyone's Money Book. 2d ed., Jordan E. Goodman (Chicago: Dearborn Financial Publishing, 1998).

Financial Planning for Couples: How to Work Together to Build Security and Success, Adriane G. Berg ((New York: Newmarket, 1993).

Improving Your Credit and Reducing Your Debt, Gail Liberman and Alan Lavine (New York: John Wiley & Sons, 1994).

The Investment Club Book, John Wasik (New York: Warner Books, 1995).

Live Long & Profit: Wealthbuilding Strategies for Every Stage of Your Life, Kay Shirley (Chicago: Dearborn Financial Publishing, 1997).

The Living Together Kit, Toni Ihara and Ralph Warner (Berkeley, Calif.: Nolo Press, 1997).

Making the Most of Your Money, Jane Bryant Quinn (New York: Simon & Schuster, 1991).

Money Advice for Your Successful Remarriage, Patricia Schiff Estess (Cincinnati, Ohio: Betterway Books, 1996).

Money Harmony, Olivia Mellan (New York: Walker and Company, 1994).

The New Century Family Money Book, Jonathan D. Pond (New York: Dell, 1995).

The Three Career Couple, Marcia Byalick and Linda Saslow, (Princeton, N.J.: Petersons, 1993).

What Every Woman Should Know About Her Husband's Money, Shelby White (New York: Random House, 1992).

The Will Kit, John Ventura (Chicago: Dearborn Financial Publishing, 1996).

The Working Parents Help Book, Susan Crites Price and Tom Price (Princeton, N.J.: Peterson's, 1994).

Your Life Insurance Options, Alan Lavine (New York: John Wiley & Sons, 1993).

Index